IS MAN
INCOMPREHENSIBLE
TO MAN?

IS MAN
INCOMPREHENSIBLE
TO MAN?

Philip H. Rhinelander

STANFORD UNIVERSITY

Trade distributor: Charles Scribner's Sons, New York

W. H. FREEMAN AND COMPANY
San Francisco

Library of Congress Cataloging in Publication Data

Rhinelander, Philip H.
    Is man incomprehensible to man?

    Reprint of the 1973 ed. published by Stanford Alumni Association,
Stanford, Calif., in series: The Portable Stanford.
    Bibliography: p.
    1. Man.   I. Title.
BD450.R445   1974   128'.3   74-8626
ISBN 0-7167-0765-9
ISBN 0-7167-0764-0 (pbk.)

Printed in the United States of America

1   2   3   4   5   6   7   8   9

If men cannot refer to a common value,
recognized by all as existing in each one,
then man is incomprehensible to man.

Camus, *The Rebel*

This book was published
originally as a part of
The Portable Stanford,
a series of books published by
the Stanford Alumni Association.

CONTENTS

ILLUSTRATIONS

Illustrations were researched with the gracious cooperation of the Stanford University Art Library.

PREFACE

My intention in writing *Is Man Incomprehensible to Man?* was to write an essay that is impressionistic rather than rigorous, and to write for the layman rather than for the professional philosopher. Hence I have tried to avoid technical discussions. It was also my intention to bring together a range of problems that are usually treated separately. Although each of the problems I have taken up in the book deserves much deeper analysis than can be accomplished in a short space, perhaps it is appropriate that what is planned as a sketch be attempted in a short space. My hope is that this essay will encourage the reader to do further reading and further thinking on his own.

It is my conviction that every person is his own philosopher insofar as he tries to think carefully, critically, and coherently about the problems of human existence. I believe too that an important mission of philosophy (and so, of everyone who would be his own philosopher) is to identify and clarify those underlying questions—often called "metaphysical" questions—which are generally ignored today as if they were unworthy of attention. The truth is that we cannot avoid making metaphysical assumptions about the world and the place of human beings in it; if we turn away from such topics, we succeed only in hiding the nature of our assumptions and leaving them unexamined.

A central theme of this study is the great influence exerted upon our thinking by metaphors, models, and analogies—especially by the ones that have become so familiar that we are unaware of their existence. In any kind of thinking, confusion arises when we employ ideal models (of which there are many kinds) without trying to make clear precisely *what* models we are using. The difficulties become especially acute when our thinking deals with "human nature," or "man," because there is no consensus today about the human nature of human existence and no likelihood of achieving consensus until we become aware at least of the variety of different models upon which we depend and of the vast difference in their implications. It seems evident that different assumptions or models of *man* lead naturally to different views about history, society, ethics, religion, art, and science.

Recent developments in various fields are converging, I think, toward a new model of human *knowing*, that, by stressing the element of *inventiveness*, offers a prospect of solving some of contemporary man's serious and persistent difficulties.

For the sake of simplicity and readability, all references have been removed from the text. However, for those who may be interested in looking further into the authors cited or quoted, a section of notes is appended at the end of the text, keyed to chapters and pages. There is also a reader's guide in which works likely to be of interest to the general reader are specially designated.

Stanford, California   *Philip H. Rhinelander*
March 1974

IS MAN
INCOMPREHENSIBLE
TO MAN?

WHO IS MAN?

"POLITICAL THEORY which does not start from a theory of man is in my view quite worthless." So wrote the British historian Hugh Trevor-Roper in 1953. The late David Potter, a distinguished American historian and a valued member of the Stanford faculty, extended the same principle to the writing of history generally. All historians, he said, necessarily make assumptions about man, whose history they are recounting, but they seldom bother to make clear what figure of man they are employing.

I should wish to make the point even more broadly. Not only political theory and history, but also theories of knowledge, theories of value, theories of ethics, theories of art, theories of language, and theories of religion depend on assumptions about *man*. Yet the crucial underlying assumptions often remain unspecified. If there were a tacit consensus about the nature of man—if some paradigm or model of man were generally accepted today—the failure to specify what model of man is being invoked on a particular occasion by a particular writer or speaker would not be a source of serious concern. But the fact is that there is no agreement today on the meaning of phrases like "human nature" or the "nature of man," or even on whether they mean anything at all. Yet we continue to invoke the concept of man in many forms of discourse, sometimes explicitly but more often tacitly, as if no need for clarification existed. I believe this circumstance directly contributes to that "crisis of values" about which so many of us are now desperately concerned.

In our modern secularized society, I think most people would accept the famous dictum of Protagoras, the ancient Greek sophist, that man is the measure of all things. But what do we really mean, after all? Do we mean that each individual is the measure of what is right for him— which is what Plato took Protagoras to be asserting? Or are we invoking some universal essence or archetype of human nature, as Plato (in effect) did? Are we talking about the average man in some particular community, whose opinions and behavior are to be determined statistically by sociological investigation? Are we invoking some model of typical man, like the famous model of Renaissance Man pictured by the historian Jacob Burckhardt—a model that did not correspond exactly with any known individual of the period but presented a composite type? Or are we thinking of an ideal model of the ethically good man, who for Aristotle was the proper measure of all genuine human good? Obviously there are many different possibilities. And only confusion can result if we talk about "man" or "the nature of man" without specifying what assumptions we are making and what we mean by such terms.

That there is at least a general correlation between our assumptions about the nature of man and our ethical and political outlook can be shown by a few examples. If, for example, we believe that all men are by nature egotistical and aggressively self-seeking, we may then conclude that men can be ruled only by force, and that an authoritarian state is necessary to provide any semblance of peace and security. Such was (in substance) the position of the eminent seventeenth-century British philosopher Thomas Hobbes. If, on the contrary, we believe that men are naturally peaceable and benevolent, and that aggressive, competitive egotism is the product of artificial restraints imposed by society, we may readily conclude that social and legal restraints on individual conduct are counterproductive and should be removed or at least minimized. Several versions of this view are held today.

Again, if we accept Freud's view that the structure of the human psyche is such that fundamental tensions are inevitable both within the individual self and between the individual and society, we may hold that our best aim is not the reform of the state or society but the securing of individual adjustment to social realities. But if we deny that the psychic constitution of individuals is thus prestructured and insist rather that human nature is indefinitely malleable, we encounter two schools of thought that agree on the general proposition, but argue in opposite directions. Jean-Paul Sartre, the well-known French author and philosopher, claimed (at least in his earlier writings) that each individual establishes his own fundamental character entirely by his own free choices. This view invites the conclusion that any submission by the individual to socially imposed norms is a betrayal of human authenticity, an act of "bad faith." But if we believe, as does B. F. Skinner, the eminent behavioral psychologist, that every individual is shaped in all essential particulars solely by environmental conditioning, then we must see free choice as a myth, and conclude that human welfare can be produced only by systematic social and psychological engineering.

What I mean to point out here, and to take up in more detail later, is simply that ambiguous assumptions about man lead to all kinds of confusion, some of which occur in our ordinary discourse. Consider, for a moment, the repeated assertion that modern technological society is dehumanizing. We take it for granted that dehumanization is bad, but how often do we stop to inquire just what is involved?

Plainly, if someone asserts that modern technology is dehumanizing, he cannot mean that technology is non-human or inhuman in its origins, since technology is a distinctively human invention. Nor can he be seriously claiming that those who live under technology have ceased to be human beings, for if that were the case the question of "dehumanization" could scarcely arise. Evidently, then, when somebody says that technology is dehumanizing, he is invoking an ideal model of what he thinks human nature *ought to be.* He is saying, in effect, that technology (or some aspects of it) prevents the full realization of human potential. So far, so good. I believe that most ethical judgments appeal to *ideal* models of man or society. But when an ideal model is invoked, it is essential that the *nature* of the model be specified. Otherwise, there _Jesus_ is no way of knowing what is meant, and no way of determining whether, or how far, the assertion may be valid. Yet such specification is almost never found. Words like *dehumanized* and *dehumanizing* have been converted, by frequent and uncritical use, into empty catchwords that do more to becloud important issues than to clarify them.

That men are susceptible to slogans and catchwords is of course a persistent fact, of which both statesmen and demagogues have taken advantage since the beginnings of recorded history. But in our day this susceptibility seems to have increased remarkably. One contributing factor, without doubt, has been the influence of the mass media and mass advertising, which value immediate impact on the audience more than the eliciting of thoughtful comprehension. But other factors seem to have been at work. Just as there is no present consensus about the nature of man, there is no consensus about the nature of modern American society. Writers of avowedly "revolutionary" sympathies like Herbert Marcuse, for example, tell us that our society is monolithic, conformist, repressive, resistant to novelty, and fundamentally opposed to serious change. The inevitable product of our society is, in his phrase, "One-Dimensional Man." We may note that in the arts apologists for the *avant-garde* have preached a parallel doctrine for several decades past, rebelling against the stultifying restrictions of "bourgeois" conventionality.

Meanwhile others assure us, with equal fervor, that modern technological society is dedicated wholly to the cult of novelty and change. Victor Ferkiss, in his book entitled *Technological Man*, asserts that "never before in human history has a civilization been so intoxicated with change." Alvin Toffler's recent best seller, *Future Shock*, warns of the dangerous stresses we encounter from our need to readjust constantly to rapid shifts in our ways of living and our social outlook. And psychologist Robert Jay Lifton reports the emergence in our day of a new psychological type, which he calls "Protean Man," who moves with relative ease from one kind of ideological orientation to another, to meet altered circumstances.

Which of these divergent interpretations is more nearly correct? Is our society firmly opposed to change, or is it intoxicated with change? Or does it fall somewhere between? Is it producing "one-dimensional" men, or "protean" men, or possibly both? To settle questions of such magnitude is beyond the scope of an essay such as this, but it is important to notice how reliance on rhetoric and jargon (notably, I think, in the case of Marcuse, whom I shall discuss later) has contributed to the tangling of the issues.

My main aim is to show that *important confusions exist concerning the nature of man and that they infect our discussions at many levels.* I believe that serious efforts at conceptual clarification are necessary. I also wish to suggest that *recent developments in a number of different fields seem to be converging toward a new view of man*—man as inventor—which offers some prospect of solving a number of difficulties, or at least of setting them in a new perspective. My treatment will necessarily be impressionistic and in many aspects superficial. But, then, I am not setting out to present the reader with a ready-made philosophical position to be adopted or rejected *en bloc*. I hope rather to invite the reader to engage in critical thinking for himself. I share the view of Karl Jaspers that philosophy consists primarily in the process of *philosophizing*. By this definition, we are all philosophers insofar as we try *to think critically and coherently about important problems and especially about our habitual ways of dealing with them.*

CHAPTER ONE

SOME VITAL ISSUES

AFTER WORLD WAR II France suffered through a peculiarly difficult period of readjustment and recovery. The joy of national liberation was dulled by the nagging memory of prior national collapse and by the realization that France had been delivered from Nazi occupation chiefly by the efforts of her allies. The relief of peace after the long catastrophe of war was troubled by the emergence, in the last days of the armed struggle, of the atomic bomb, which hung over the whole world as a harbinger of ultimate doom. Moves toward the reestablishment of internal order included—naturally and perhaps necessarily—efforts to expose and punish those who had collaborated with the occupying Germans. But just as the collaborators themselves had acted in a variety of ways with a variety of motives, so did their avengers. And the results were often chaotic and inconsistent. Some major malefactors went unpunished or escaped with minimal penalties while, at the other extreme, innocent people were punished for alleged collaboration on charges manufactured out of spite to fit the passions and resentments of the times.

Reflecting on such conditions, the French author Gabriel Marcel wrote a book called *Man Against Mass Society* that is deserving of our attention, because it so cogently speaks to the question of the philosopher's mission in a world marked by spreading violence and passionate confusions. To be sure, the problems of America in the 1970s are not identical with those of France in the late 1940s. But this does not mean that there may not be common patterns of malaise. And it should be noted that though Marcel's observations were prompted by a particular historical situation in a particular country, he was writing, not specifically about France or the attitudes of Frenchmen in the 1940s, but about Western man at mid-century. I can find no better point of departure than to present Marcel's views on five issues I wish to discuss.

One: On Man's Idea of Himself

"Man depends, to a very great degree, on the idea he has of himself," says Marcel, "and . . . this idea cannot be degraded without at the same time degrading man." This remark calls attention to an important distinction, habitually overlooked by those who believe that we should aim to establish a "science" of man according to the model of a science of physical nature. No man by taking thought can add a cubit to his stature or alter the laws of physics and chemistry. But he can, by taking thought—or accepting other people's thought—modify his own ways of thinking and acting. There is, therefore, a kind of feedback effect between *theories* of human nature and human behavior itself. For this reason, Leon Eisenberg, a psychiatrist, speaks of theories of human nature as having the character of *self-fulfilling prophecies*. In an article in *Science* (April 14, 1972) on "The Human Nature of Human Nature," Eisenberg writes:

> The planets will move as they always have, whether we adopt a geocentric or a heliocentric view of the heavens. . . . The motions of the planets are sublimely indifferent to our earth-bound astronomy. But the behavior of man is not independent of the theories of human behavior that men adopt. . . .
>
> What we believe of man affects the behavior of men, for it determines what each expects of the other. Theories of education, of political science, of economics, and the very policies of governments are based on implicit concepts of the nature of man. Is he educable? Is he actuated only by self-interest? Is he a creature of such dark lusts that only submission to sovereign authority can save him from himself?
>
> What we choose to believe about the nature of man has social consequences. These consequences should be weighed in assessing the belief we choose to hold, even provisionally,

given the lack of compelling proof for any of the currently fashionable theories. . . . The thrust of my argument is that there is no solid foundation to the theoretical extrapolation of the instinctivists, the ethologists, the behaviorists, *or the* psychoanalysts despite the special pleading that often is so seductive to those eager for a "real science" of behavior. Further to the point, belief helps shape actuality because of the self-fulfilling character of social prophecy. . . . Pessimism about man serves to maintain the status quo. . . . No less clearly, the false "optimism" of the unsubstantiated claims made for behavioral engineering, claims that ignore biological variations and individual creativity, foreclose man's humanity.

The last sentence seems to be directed chiefly against behaviorists like B. F. Skinner, who does not merely ignore but has explicitly rejected the notion of human creativity. I shall return to this topic later. For now the point I want to make is that the ideas men have about the nature of man have practical consequences for behavior.

Two: On the Need for Metaphysical Understanding

Marcel insists that "the crisis which Western man is undergoing today is a metaphysical one. . . . There is probably no more dangerous illusion than that of imagining that some readjustment of social or institutional conditions could suffice of itself to appease a contemporary sense of disquiet which rises, in fact, from the very depth of man's being." But he immediately insists that he does not mean that the existence of a metaphysical crisis should be used as a justification for social inertia. His aim is rather to facilitate analysis, which, in his view, is endangered by "political preoccupations falsifying all discussions, all honest attempts at analysis." I think Marcel's position here might be paraphrased by citing this prayer (ascribed to Reinhold Niebuhr): "God grant me the serenity to accept the things I cannot change, the courage to change the things I can, and the wisdom to know the difference." The crucial element is the third—wisdom to know the difference.

Human thought on the subject of social change seems generally to oscillate between two extremes. Either it is assumed that *everything* must always be as it has been and now is, with the result that no effort is made to reduce familiar evils of poverty, violence, and injustice; or it is assumed, with bursting confidence in the perfectibility of man, that *all* human evils can be eliminated by socio-economic restructuring, by political change, by technological advance, or by a combination of the three. Marcel holds that both views are dangerously mistaken. There are many human evils that can be eliminated or reduced. But there are others inherent in the human condition itself, and since these cannot be escaped as long as man is man, they must be borne. If this is the case— as I believe it is—then our first task is to distinguish between the two types.

The crisis that Marcel calls "metaphysical" is associated (in large measure) with what Viktor Frankl has called "man's search for meaning." I shall discuss this topic later, and shall argue that the search for order and meaning in human existence has been a persistent theme in literature, philosophy, and religion from the earliest times. The Book of Job was a classic statement of the problem as it arose in the context of religious monotheism. But metaphysics has been out of fashion in the Western world for some time past, owing largely, I believe, to the complacent faith in unending growth and automatic progress that characterized Western thought through the nineteenth century and down to the first World War. When blind optimism is destroyed, the natural result is apt to be a violent swing to the opposite extreme—blind pessimism, which is equally impatient with efforts at rational analysis of complex problems. As Walter Kaufmann, of Princeton, puts it: "The new anti-faith in the unique alienation of modern man is as unsound and unsophisticated as the old faith in progress. The notion that things were never so good and are constantly getting better, and the notion that things were never so bad and are steadily getting worse, are entirely worthy of each other." Perhaps the way is now being cleared for the kind of honest analysis of metaphysical problems that Marcel believed essential.

Three: On the Importance of Historical Understanding

For Marcel, "one of the duties of a philosopher, if he shows himself worthy of his vocation today, is to attack quite directly those dissimulating forces which are all working toward what might be called a neutralization of the past; and whose conjoint effort consists in arousing in contemporary man a feeling of what I should like to call insulation in time." We ought to aim rather, he thinks, "at a restoration of that unity of poetic vision and philosophic creativity of which the great pre-Socratic philosophers offer us one of the first known examples."

The American ethos has been non-historical, if not anti-historical, for many generations. Americans have characteristically looked to the future, not the past. They have seen America as a country dedicated to transcending the limitations of Old World traditions toward new beginnings, new horizons of opportunity, and a new birth of freedom in the overcoming of new frontiers. Henry Ford's classic observation that "history is more or less bunk" reflected—on a lower intellectual level —the same optimistic faith in practicality, the same trust in the possibility of unlimited growth and progress, and the same distrust of abstract knowledge separated from concrete action that animated the philosophy of John Dewey. The result has been a climate of opinion in which history, though accepted as an academic subject, has been held in slight value in the popular culture. It is thus not altogether surprising to find that the "irrelevance" of history has become an article of faith among many radical students, since middle-class student "radicals" frequently exemplify the tacit views of the society that they claim to reject.

In January 1969, *Fortune* magazine published a special issue on student unrest, which later became the book *Youth in Turmoil*. Among the materials in the book is an essay called "An American Student Manifesto," described by the editors as containing a distillation of some two hundred interviews with students on a score of campuses. On the subject of historical studies, the students were quoted as believing:

> We have only begun to experiment. Gradually, we are shedding the prejudices with which we entered school. Our critics accuse us of not learning from history and, therefore, as Santayana's dictum puts it, of being condemned to repeat it. But we say that there is no historical precedent for our generation. Never before has there been a country rich enough to take care of its entire population, nor a generation of youth so thoroughly molded and controlled by the power structure.

Here are two statements that, however paradoxical, are surely familiar to anyone acquainted with the American campus scene in the late 1960s. One is the dramatic assertion that the protesting generation is "thoroughly molded and controlled by the power structure." If this dogma were true, it is hard to see how any substantial protest against the "power structure" could have arisen or spread so widely. We are told, in effect, that there is student protest because student protest is impossible. And this assertion is bracketed with the further claim that history is of no concern *because* there is "no historical precedent" for the present situation. One might justly ask how the absence of historical precedent can be determined without historical study. We are assured, however, that by *presupposing what history might show* if we looked we are spared the trouble of looking.

What emerges is an obvious case of the modern "insulation in time" and the "neutralization of the past" against which Marcel protested, a failure to recognize that history is our best source of information about the nature of man. For whatever the cultural context, and whatever the specific problems from epoch to epoch, *man* is still the constant, and we can learn more about man when we consider how he has behaved under differing circumstances than we could learn by confining our attention to one particular set.

Four: On Moral Commitment and the Nature of Fanaticism

Marcel insists that "the first duty of the philosopher in our world today is to fight against fanaticism *under whatever guise it may appear.*" He contends that fanaticism is rooted in "slavery to words," and that such slavery, together with the fanaticism it often engenders, reflects a "spirit of abstraction," which he identifies with the passions and emotions rather than with the intellect. The dynamic element in his philosophy, Marcel asserts in his Preface, can be seen as "an obstinate and untiring battle against the spirit of abstraction"—for this, he holds, is a primary factor making for war and violence.

I believe that Marcel's analysis throws important light on many current problems, especially if we bear in mind the observation of Yves Simon that whereas fanaticism was once associated with ideological certitude and the pursuit of absolute commitments, we now know that it may also arise from agnosticism and resentful doubt.

Five: On the Mission of the Philosopher

In Marcel's view, the charge of the philosopher in today's world is not to take stands on particular contemporary political and social issues, but to cut deeper by working in all areas and on all issues for honesty, openness, and "a certain noble and generous simplicity in the fundamental human relationships," and against *all* forces that threaten to destroy the love of life or to debase the "dignity of man."

> There can be no question here of my attempting to define anything at all resembling a political line of action. What we have to do with is rather an inner attitude; but this inner attitude cannot remain at the stage of mere attitude; it must find expression in deeds, and that according to the situation in which each of us finds himself: I mean by that, that this is not a mat-

ter, as is unfortunately so often the habit of intellectuals, of our thrusting ourselves into fields in which we are wholly without authority, by signing appeals, manifestos, and so on. ... But on the other hand it is within the scope of each of us, within his own proper field, in his profession, to pursue an unrelaxing struggle for man, for the dignity of man, against everything that today threatens to annihilate man and his dignity.

Again, he insists that the pervasive enemy is devotion to *abstractions,* which are mistaken for concrete reality.

A philosopher who made a claim . . . to speak only in terms of the absolute would at the same time totally disqualify himself from having a relevant contribution to make to any concrete problem. And, very generally, we *can* say that nothing is more characteristic than the incredible blindness of professors of philosophy when they decide to take a stand on political questions. One recognizes in them a spirit of rashness which can be explained . . . by the simple fact that unlike doctors, architects or engineers, they are in contact chiefly with words and ideas and hardly ever with things. The illusion that one is flying is a melancholy one in the case of a man who does not even know how to walk and, for that matter, rather despises walking.

This position is, of course, highly controversial, since (as Marcel realized) it runs counter to the prevailing impulse toward intellectual activism. But Marcel's view is worth taking seriously because of this very fact. I take him to be saying two things. First, unless we have a reasonably clear idea of man as he *is,* as he *might be,* and as he *should be,* we cannot distinguish between those evils that can be modified or eliminated and those evils that are intrinsic to the human condition and must be borne. If we cannot make this distinction, and if we have no settled ideal of man toward which to work, we subject ourselves to the deepening clash of partial and passionate views, generating heat rather than light, obscuring fundamental issues, and encouraging the very "dehumanization" of man that everybody claims to be seeking to avoid. Second, he is putting forward an ideal of the philosophic character as exemplifying certain general traits or dispositions of mind, including simplicity, honesty, openness, wisdom, humility, and generosity. There is an echo here—indeed, more than an echo—of the classical ideal of the philosopher, along with clear recognition of the fact that such a stance is peculiarly difficult to maintain, especially in time of crisis when it is most needed. Marcel saw quite clearly that "the philosophic spirit is bound to see itself slandered both by the fanatic and the false prophet, who in the long run always runs the risk of himself becoming fanaticized."

It will be observed that these issues are not new. Witness Thucydides' comments on the effects of civil strife and revolution at Corcyra during the Peloponnesian War:

> Words changed their ordinary meanings and were construed in new senses. Reckless daring passed for the courage of a loyal partisan, far-sighted caution was regarded as the excuse of a coward, moderation was taken to be the pretext of the unmanly, the power to see all sides of a question was seen as complete inability to act. Impulsive rashness was held to be the mark of a man, caution in planning was a specious excuse for avoiding action. A violent attitude was always to be trusted, its opponents were suspect. . . .
>
> So civil war gave birth to every kind of iniquity in the Greek world. Simplicity, the chief ingredient in a noble nature, was ridiculed and disappeared, and society was divided into rival camps in which no man trusted his fellow.

What has changed in our day is not the pattern of human conduct in time of crisis, for Thucydides' description could apply today. It is rather that the modern concept of *moderation* has acquired connotations very different from the classical view of balanced judgment and the need to find the mean between extremes. As Lon Fuller of Harvard has observed, Aristotle's concept of the mean is not to be confused with the modern notion of the *middle way*: "For moderns the middle way is the easy way, involving a minimum of commitment. For Aristotle the mean was the hard way, the way from which the slothful and unskilled were most likely to fall."

Man the Wayfarer

These, then, are the five issues, or sets of issues, that I shall discuss in the remainder of this book. Before proceeding further, however, let me explain why I have chosen Gabriel Marcel's views as a point of departure. This was partly a matter of convenience, since *Man Against Mass Society* puts forth the issues with which I wish primarily to deal. But there is also a further consideration. Marcel is not an academic philosopher. He belongs to no "school." Although popularly classed as a religious existentialist, he came to repudiate the label existentialist because of its misleading connotations, while recognizing that his thinking has notable affinities with (as well as differences from) several existentialist writers who are better known. He defies classification, being a dramatist whose plays are, in a sense, metaphysical and a thinker whose philosophical writings are, in a sense, dramatic. For him, as for Jaspers, philosophy is the activity of philosophizing. Reflective thinking (as practiced by Marcel) does not separate thought from feeling, much less does it consist of making oracular pronouncements or setting up abstract systems. Instead, thinking becomes a kind of feeling and acting—an encountering of human reality and human suffering on a plane that combines intelligence with sympathy and understanding. (I use the word *understanding* here in the sense in which it is used in the French proverb that to understand all is to forgive, although I would insist that to forgive is not to approve.)

Marcel entitled one of his books *Homo Viator* (Man the Wayfarer) and I think the designation is apt for Marcel himself. A wayfarer is neither a tourist nor a geographer nor (primarily) a pathfinder, but a traveler on beaten paths. Marcel's philosophical writings—which are impressionistic rather than systematic—are informed by the same aspiration that he once described as the main function of the theater, "not to relate the particular to the general or to a law or to an idea, but to awaken or re-awaken in us the consciousness of the infinite which is concealed in the particular." And, he added, with reference to the theatrical audience, "I am sure that the desired metaphysical impetus can only come to the spectator from creatures like himself, whose experiences and problems resemble his own."

Marcel, therefore, has no professional or academic axe to grind. He is free from the two dangers that chiefly threaten the academic specialist: the pressure to conform to reigning professional conventions and the pressure to establish his own originality. I do not suppose that Marcel's views will necessarily commend themselves to all readers, but they are worth attention, at least as a starting point for the ensuing discussion.

CHAPTER TWO

LANGUAGE, METAPHORS, AND MODELS

SOME YEARS AGO Stuart Chase wrote a book called *The Tyranny of Words* in which he argued that general words are virtually, if not entirely, meaningless. His exposition might have been more persuasive if he had not had to employ general words in propounding his thesis. Thus a paradox emerged: to the extent that his arguments were persuasive, they discredited themselves. Such is the plight of anyone who tries to communicate the opinion that communication is impossible. Yet we do well to remember that communication often fails and that general terms are often deceptive.

The fact is, of course, that although language is one of the most important and remarkable of human inventions, like all human inventions it is ambivalent and double-edged. It can be used to transmit information, to extend, clarify, and preserve knowledge, to exhort and persuade, to amuse or instruct, to express emotions, and to promote mutual understanding. But it can also be used (intentionally or unintentionally) to falsify information, to obscure knowledge, to rouse passions, and to block understanding. Efforts to improve and perfect the medium, in the hope of separating the desirable functions of language from the undesirable functions, may have limited usefulness for specialized purposes, but a language sufficiently rich, flexible, and forceful for normal use is inevitably subject to misuse. The problem is not with language as such, but with the speakers or writers who employ it. As Hobbes remarked, "Words are the counters of wise men, but the money of fools."

Linguistic Confusion and the Quest for Clarity

The potential misuse of language has concerned man since the time of the Classical Greeks. Socrates condemned the sophists of his day because they were more concerned with teaching their pupils how to manipulate an audience by persuasive rhetoric than with presenting the truth. He was also acutely aware of the confusions engendered, even for honest minds, by familiar words, especially when used uncritically. Many of the Socratic dialogues center upon the need to find viable definitions of particular words, like *justice* and *piety*. What Socrates was seeking might better be termed conceptual clarification, but the fact remains that he was sensitive to the difficulties posed by the uncritical use of general words, which are often taken to be clear simply because they are in general circulation.

Familiar symbols, whether verbal or nonverbal, typically acquire strong symbolic associations—intellectual or emotional, or both. It is chiefly this fact which gives words their force, and which makes possible the effective use of metaphor. But sometimes the symbolic association attached to a word can distort or even reverse the significance of the particular facts that the word is used to describe or designate. Our sense of fact, or what we call *reality*, is often overcome by misdescriptions, particularly if they are put forward with apparent authority or if they achieve wide acceptance. The familiar tale of the Emperor's new clothes is a case in point.

Indeed, some recent philosophers have been led to assert that all philosophical claims are essentially claims about language. In this view, philosophy consists simply of "talk about talk." Such a position can lead easily to the further view that many, if not all, of the traditional problems of philosophy, notably metaphysical problems, are *created* by the misuse of language and may be solved—or more properly dissolved—when the underlying linguistic confusions are exposed. This position, though perhaps less influential today than it was ten or twenty years ago, is still sufficiently entrenched to call for comment. I consider it mistaken for several reasons.

In the first place it tacitly converts a theoretical claim about the "logic" of language into a psychological claim about the origins of philosophical inquiry and the psychological grounds of intellectual bewilderment and error. To assert that men are typically impelled toward metaphysical speculation because of confusions over language is to make a factual claim requiring empirical (i.e., psychological or anthropological) evidence in its support. But such evidence has not been offered. Nor does it seem to be available. It is clearly established, for example, that tribal societies have been universally concerned with myth, magic, and religion. To suggest that their concerns were prompted by lingustic errors plainly seems absurd; on the contrary, the magical and ritual observances of primitive tribes appear to have been among the earliest forms of symbolic representation from which language systems also took their origin. Alfred North Whitehead is quite right, I believe, in asserting that "human life is driven forward by its dim apprehension of notions too general for its existing language." The historical process, then, seems to be one in which language brings to light conceptual problems or conceptual inadequacies, prompting the development of new concepts and thus progressively enriching the language. Many examples of such *conceptual evolution* reflected in verbal changes have been traced, for example, in Greek thought.

The second difficulty with the "language governs all" approach is that, if we are to dismiss certain kinds of inquiry or certain types of bewilderment as illegitimate, we must set up some norm or standard by which to judge between acceptable questions and unacceptable questions—or, as it is sometimes phrased, between genuine problems and pseudo-problems. In search of such a norm, three procedures have been used. The first has been to take that *branch of knowledge* in which the highest degree of clarity and certainty has been achieved and apply it as a standard for all other areas. This was the procedure of René Descartes, who envisioned the ideal of a universal mathematics that would be applicable in all fields of inquiry. He proposed that "only those objects should engage our attention, to the sure and indubitable knowledge of which our mental powers seem to be adequate." It is not that arithmetic and geometry are the only sciences to be studied, he added, but simply that "in our search for the direct road toward the truth *we should busy ourselves with no object about which we cannot attain a certitude equal to that of the demonstration of Arithmetic and Geometry.*" (Italics added.) The effect of this procedure is to redefine the word *knowledge* by stipulating that nothing should count as knowledge unless it satisfies a specific model borrowed from one particular field and, at the same time, to rule out any questions not susceptible to being answered with the same degree of certainty and precision prescribed by the chosen model.

This procedure of Descartes has been extremely influential. Modern empiricists, notably the logical positivists, have modified Descartes' rule by broadening the model to include the standard procedures of empirical science, but they follow Descartes in thinking it proper to take the methods and results of certain particular fields of inquiry as an ideal model for *all* fields and to reject as illegitimate (or meaningless) all questions and all forms of inquiry that fail to fit the paradigm. The result is a kind of dogmatic intellectual Puritanism, thoroughly *unempirical* in nature, which has been largely responsible for the widespread neglect in our day of metaphysical and ethical questions because they cannot be handled "scientifically."

Aristotle, in fact, warned against this very mistake, contending that "the same exactness [sought in science] must not be expected in all departments of philosophy alike. . . . It is the mark of an educated mind to expect that amount of exactness in each kind [of inquiry] which the nature of the particular subject admits. It is equally unreasonable to accept merely probable conclusions from a mathematician, and to demand strict demonstrations from an orator." I think that Aristotle was obviously right. The irony is that the positivists have invoked an ideal model of human knowledge to discredit inquiry concerning ideal models of human nature and conduct.

A second procedure for establishing a standard by which to rule out illegitimate philosophical inquiries has been directed toward constructing *ideal languages* that would guarantee logical clarity and neutralize the effect of symbolic associations attached to particular words. But however useful such languages may be for special kinds of inquiry, they have thus far proved wholly inadequate to meet the many needs of ordinary discourse.

A third approach consists in taking *ordinary language* as the controlling standard of legitimate discourse. The analysis of ordinary language has produced useful results in calling attention to the many different ways in which words are used, and in reminding us of important distinctions and tacit assumptions that we actually make but often overlook when we engage in abstract theoretical discussions. The ordinary language philosophers have commendably attacked pretentious jargon and demanded simplicity. But the appeal to ordinary language has sometimes been used as a pretext for treating empirical or ontological assumptions about matters of fact as if they were established by the "logic" of our talk about them or as a supposed basis for choosing between alternate ways of describing phenomena where both are used in common speech.

J. L. Austin, the most careful student of ordinary language, concludes that although ordinary language may properly be taken as the "first word"—that is, as the best starting point for philosophical anal-

ysis—it "has no claim to be the last word, if there is such a thing." Thus we are brought to the position of Socrates. As Whitehead puts it: "Philosophy is a difficult subject, from the days of Plato to the present time haunted by subtle perplexities. The existence of such perplexities arising from the obviousness of speech is the reason why the topic exists. Thus the very purpose of philosophy is to delve below the apparent clarity of common speech. In this connection, it is only necessary to refer to Socrates."

Metaphor, Analogy, and an "Eye for Resemblances"

I have said that the force of words, like other symbols, is linked to their capacity to acquire symbolic associations. In this connection, it is appropriate to say a few words on the topic of metaphor, analogy, and conceptual models, which play a much more fundamental role in our thinking than is usually recognized.

Aristotle recognized the importance of metaphor in poetry, observing that "command of metaphor . . . is the mark of genius, for to make good metaphors implies an eye for resemblances." But he regarded metaphor simply as a special ornament of literary style, involving a departure from common usage. This conception of metaphor has persisted, and many of us take it for granted that metaphorical language is a kind of decoration that may be appropriate to the arts but has no place in the sciences or in the matter-of-fact and literal discourse we employ in common life when we are concerned with exchanging information.

It lately has come to be recognized, however, that metaphor and analogy—which suggest, as Aristotle said, an "eye for resemblances"—are involved in all types of thinking, including scientific thinking. This fact is reflected in our vocabulary. Most of the words we use to describe intellectual operations, for example, are clearly metaphorical in origin, having been borrowed from physical or physiological happenings. When we speak of sense "impressions," for instance, we are employing the old analogy of the signet ring impressing its form on the wax. When we use terms like *insight, foresight, vision,* or *perspicacity* to denote intelligence in contrast to the *blindness* of stupidity, or when we speak of *enlightenment* or *illumination* to denote knowledge, or when we contrast a *bright* student with a *dull* student, we are linking intellectual knowledge to the process of visual perception. The *optical model of knowledge,* with its associated images of light and darkness, is notably pervasive and persistent. Words like *theory* and *idea* are derived from Greek words associated originally with visual perception.

Hans Jonas has argued plausibly that the optical model of mind, which has been so generally accepted that it has embedded itself in our very language, lies at the root of our concept of "objectivity" and has contributed to our difficulties with the concept of causality, since we *see* physical objects without apparently affecting them but do not *see* the actual operation of causal efficacy or agency.

Examples could be multiplied to show the operation of metaphor and analogy in the development of scientific thought. The early view that electricity behaves like a liquid—a view that was temporarily fruitful—has left its impression on our vocabulary: we speak of electric *current* and often describe it as *flowing*, both these terms involving a metaphorical extension of words originally applied to other phenomena. The idea that the universe might be conceived after the model of a vast mechanical clock that God had created and left to run by itself—a concept that was basic to the mechanistic view elaborated by Descartes and Newton—has been traced back to Nicholas Oremus, Bishop of Lisieux, who died more than two centuries before Descartes was born. It was, according to Lynn White, Jr., "a notion with a future: eventually the metaphor became a metaphysics."

Thought as Metaphor

These examples are sufficient, I believe, to confirm I. A. Richard's criticism of the traditional view of metaphor: "The traditional theory noticed only a few of the modes of metaphor and limited its application of the term *metaphor* to a few of them only. And thereby it made metaphor seem to be a verbal matter, a shifting and displacement of words; whereas, fundamentally it is a borrowing between and intercourse of *thoughts*, a transaction between contexts. *Thought* is metaphoric, and proceeds by comparison, and the metaphors of language derive therefrom."

The implications are of great importance. Philosophers of language have tried to achieve clarity of discourse by carefully distinguishing and cataloguing the different "senses" in which particular words are regularly used. But the inherently metaphorical character of thought and language creates serious difficulties, since words are continually subject to extension in their application, and this very flexibility is an important factor in the usefulness of speech. The savage seeing an airplane for the first time naturally calls it a bird, thereby assimilating it to that object of his own experience to which it is most similar. When the automobile was first introduced, it was often referred to as a "horseless carriage," a phrase that might seem to involve a contradiction in terms if the word *carriage* were tied rigidly to its original sense.

Whenever we are confronted by a new phenomenon or a new (or newly recognized) state of affairs, our first impulse is to assimilate it to the models and categories to which we are accustomed. It is only later, after anomalies have come to light, that we face the need to construct new models or to set up new categories, with appropriate modifications or extensions of our common vocabulary and idiom, to accommodate the new conditions. If the forms of language did not allow for this kind of analogical or metaphorical extension of customary terminology—to be followed later by adjustments in the interest of clarity and coherence—language would lose one of its chief values. We should find ourselves locked into a rigid conceptual and linguistic frame immune to change or development of any kind.

To those who would object that this process is "irrational," let me say that such an objection appears to presuppose that rationality is tied to the particular form of reasoning in which we take universal statements ("All men are mortal") and on the basis of other statements ("Socrates is a man") proceed to deduce conclusions ("Socrates is mortal"). But the process of subsuming a particular case (or set of cases) under a general rule does not exhaust our powers of discursive reasoning. We can deal with ratios and proportions, holding for example that a is to b as c is to d. This is to assert no more than an identity of relationship among entities that may have nothing else in common. Analogical reasoning is of this type. The difficulty, of course, is that analogies and metaphors are incomplete. They remark the resemblance but ignore the differences. Thus they may lead us to assume an essential identity merely on the strength of a vivid but accidental similarity.

Herein lies the peculiar force of what have been called "dead" metaphors, examples of which are legion. (Consider, for a start, *fork* in the road, the *leg* of a table, the *leaf* of a book, *strong* light, *brilliant* performance, *soft* color, and *broken* heart.) A metaphor is supposedly dead—which is itself a metaphorical phrase—when it has become so generally accepted that its metaphorical character is lost to sight. The fact is, however, that if the metaphor happens to embody a pervasive model, the model may continue to operate more effectively than ever after it has become embedded in habitual usage precisely because its presence is no longer recognized. We would do better to think of such metaphors, not as dead, but as having gone underground. Take, for example, the use of *I see* for *I understand*. The use of the word *see* in this sense is well established. But it is not as innocuous as it might appear because it reaffirms and perpetuates the optical model of mind. Association of the term *imagination* with the idea of mental *images*—another metaphorical conception—has served to perpetuate the idea that beyond reproducing mental impressions from past experience, imagining is merely a kind of pretending that plays no serious part in the advancement of knowledge or understanding. As I shall argue later, I think it plain that man's most distinctive capacity is his prodigious inventiveness, which is manifested in his science, his technology, his art, his religion, his legal and political institutions, and his moral aspirations. It is even possible that, as the fable of Icarus suggested long ago, man's powers of invention are too great for his own good. However that may be, though the word *imagination* in popular parlance suggests inventiveness and creativity, it is still haunted (in much philosophical discussion) by the ghost of mental *images* and an optical model of consciousness that depicts the mind as *receptive* and *reactive* rather than innovative and constructive. Intellectual habits are hard to break, especially when they are rooted in traditional models whose existence has been forgotten.

This part of the discussion can best be brought to a focus by turning again to Richards:

> That metaphor is the omnipresent principle of language can be shown by mere observation. We cannot go through three sentences of ordinary fluid discourse without it. . . . Even in the rigid language of the settled sciences we do not eliminate it or prevent it without great difficulty. . . . In philosophy, above all, we can take no step safely without an unrelaxing awareness of the metaphors we, and our audience, may be employing; and though we may pretend to eschew them, we can attempt to do so only by detecting them. And this is the more true, the more severe and abstract the philosophy is. As it grows more abstract we think increasingly by means of metaphors that we profess *not* to be relying on. The metaphors we are avoiding steer our thought as much as those we accept.

I am not saying that we should try to get rid of models and metaphors, which would be impossible, but rather that we should be *aware* of them, so that we can appreciate both their strengths and their limitations.

CHAPTER THREE

THE DEBASEMENT OF LANGUAGE

LEWIS MUMFORD'S CHARGE that the modern age has "specialized in the debasement of language" must be taken seriously. He identifies technology and what he calls the "megamachine" as the primary culprits, but I think the matter can be put more simply. The mass media and particularly mass advertising aim at achieving an immediate impact on a large and varied audience. For this purpose the catchy slogan and the striking phrase are the most useful tools. They are designed to arrest attention, to reduce complexities to simplicities, to discourage the time-consuming process of critical reflection, and in general to elicit an immediate response that will be impervious to second thoughts. When we are aware of this kind of manipulation, we become properly skeptical, and some people have come to distrust particular sources—perhaps government spokesmen, news analysts, advertisers, or apologists for certain causes—almost as a matter of principle. Unfortunately, skepticism in one direction is often accompanied by increased credulity in others, and a disposition to doubt statements emanating from one kind of source may indicate, not an advance in critical thinking, but an uncritical devotion to the opposition.

What concerns me here, however, is not these familiar aspects of our general culture but the fact that many critics of mass culture have come to exemplify the very tendencies they claim to deplore. The disposition to accept novel and striking phrases as if they were distillations of profound wisdom has spread to the academicians and intellectuals. Indeed, it is especially disquieting that those who should be the guardians of the language, since it is their stock in trade, have contributed so notably to its deterioration.

Critics of Mass Culture and Linguistic Debasement

Consider Marshall McLuhan. In 1951 he wrote a book called *The Mechanical Bride: Folklore of Industrial Man*, a powerful assault on a culture dominated by the mass media and mass advertising. It attracted little notice. McLuhan became a celebrity only when, in his later works, he went in for catchy phrases like "the medium is the message" and "the medium is the massage," both used as titles of books that sold widely. Critics have been unable to agree on McLuhan's significance, because his writings are full of manifest inconsistencies and crammed with gnomic utterances which seem to fall apart when analyzed. Supporters of McLuhan have defended him on the ground that his writings are meant to be stimulating and that his insights are not to be judged according to accepted canons of truth and falsity. But one fact emerges clearly: to spread his thesis that in the electronic age "linear" thinking based on the printed word is obsolescent, he has used the printed word as his main vehicle of communication. What he has demonstrated (intentionally or not) is that the literate public of today has become a sucker for verbal slogans, if they are novel and arresting, and particularly if they are sufficiently incomprehensible to appear mysteriously profound.

This state of affairs should not surprise us. When advertisers have come to believe that their mission is to sell the sizzle rather than the steak, and emphasis is habitually put more on the packaging than the product, the natural consequence in the intellectual sphere is that catchwords are more valued than the ideas they are supposed to convey. McLuhan is right, I think, in believing that the electronic age has altered our customary patterns of thinking, but wrong about the nature and direction of the alteration. We face, not a growing emancipation from words, but an increased slavery to them. We should note in this connection that writing and printing are no more *linear* than speech—if anything, they are less so. When we talk we move serially from word to word and from sentence to sentence, which reflects the fact that we cannot think or talk about everything at once. Our attention, like our observation, is necessarily selective. With a written text, however, we can look back and reexamine what we have previously read; whereas spoken words, once uttered, can be recalled only by uncertain memory. In brief, the cult of McLuhan provides evidence that in a society dominated by the mass media and mass advertising, catchwords and verbal slogans, far from losing force, acquire added power as they are detached from the complexities of fact and come to operate as substitutes for thought.

Herbert Marcuse, another intellectual celebrity of recent years, took note of this fact and based his radical critique of American society largely upon it. In his best known work, *One-Dimensional Man*, Marcuse argued that the habitual repetition of standard catchwords and slogans has the effect of converting factual assertions into what philosophers call analytic propositions; that is, into self-validating verbal tautologies which are true solely by virtue of the meanings ascribed to the terms employed. Speaking of the kind of public discourse that takes place in modern America, Marcuse writes: "At the nodal points of the universe of public discourse, self-validating, analytical propositions appear which function like magic-ritual formulas. Hammered and re-hammered into the recipient's mind, they produce the effect of enclosing it within the circle of conditions prescribed by the formula."

Let me clarify this with an example of what I think Marcuse had in mind. Suppose I assert that America is a land of freedom. If I have a definition of the word *freedom* that is independent of its application to America, then I am hereby saying something significant about America which can be tested for truth or falsity by looking at actual evidence. But suppose that by constant talk of American freedom I have come to define freedom (tacitly if not explicitly) as meaning the political condition that is found in America. In this situation, to say that America is a land of freedom becomes an empty tautology; it is to say only that the political condition found in America is the political condition found in America. Such an assertion is true by definition, but it is altogether empty. An assertion of this kind masquerades as a significant statement but actually operates as nothing more than a ritual formula, a kind of verbal incantation. In recognizing the process by which uncritical repetition of familiar slogans can convert factual statements into empty tautologies and in recognizing further that current social conditions encourage this process, Marcuse seems to be on firm ground. In this aspect, his analysis is far more persuasive than McLuhan's.

But Marcuse signally fails to grasp the full import of his own analysis. Having coined the phrase "one-dimensional man" to designate the person who has become mesmerized by fashionable verbal clichés, Marcuse never asks himself whether this description might not apply to himself. The question is important, since standard leftist claims that

America is "imperialist," for example, are convertible into analytic tautologies just as readily as liberal or rightest counterclaims that America is "free." The truth is that the disease of one-dimensionality has spread everywhere. Indeed, Marcuse *exemplifies* the kind of thinking he pretends to attack. His central contention is that America is monolithic and oppressive, therefore no effective dissent is possible. This appears to be a factual claim. But Marcuse does not support it by any systematic review of evidence; instead, he tries to deduce it from a collection of heavy verbalisms borrowed partly from Hegel, partly from Marx, and partly from Freud. He relies heavily on assertions that (to borrow his own words) consist of "self-validating, analytical propositions which function like magic-ritual formulas." The fact that when such self-validating formulas are "hammered and re-hammered into the recipient's mind, they produce the effect of enclosing it within the circle of conditions prescribed by the formula" is clearly borne out by the kind of pamphleteering that Marcuse's influence has inspired. An instance may be seen in the student manifesto quoted earlier claiming that historical inquiry is irrelevant because "never before has there been a generation of youth so thoroughly molded and controlled by the power structure." This is pure Marcuse, and calls attention to one of the paradoxes in his view.

Alasdair MacIntyre, a harsh critic of Marcuse, puts the paradox bluntly:

> The central oddity of *One-Dimensional Man* is perhaps that it should have been written at all. For if its thesis were true, then we should have to ask how the book came to have been written and we should certainly have to inquire whether it would find any readers. Or rather, to the extent that the book does find readers, to that extent Marcuse's thesis does not hold. For Marcuse's thesis is that "technical progress, extended to a whole system of domination and coordination, creates forms of life (and of power) which appear to reconcile the forces opposing the system and to defeat or refute all protest in the name of the historical prospects of freedom from toil and domination." Even thought has been subordinated so that it provides no source for the criticism of social life. If social control in the interest of the *status quo* is then so powerful, how has Marcuse's book evaded this control?

Marcuse depends heavily on the associative significance of words. I myself would add merely that Marcuse's logic is reminiscent of the argument known as "Morton's Fork." Chancellor Morton, serving King Henry VII of England, argued that if a man lived sumptuously, it proved that he was rich enough to pay large taxes; whereas, if he lived poorly, it proved that he was hoarding his money and so could afford to pay large taxes. Morton's "heads, I win—tails, you lose" argument was not wholly unrelated to facts, since men who live sumptuously are usually rich and those who live meanly are sometimes misers hoarding their wealth in secret. But he was plainly not interested in determining a man's real status, since the effect of his argument was to prescribe in advance that no factual evidence could affect the conclusion. Marcuse proceeds in the same way. If capitalist industrialism prevents criticism, this proves that it is monolithic and oppressive; if it permits free criticism, this also proves that it is monolithic and oppressive because its tolerance is merely a device for drawing the teeth of the opponents. Once more, it is heads, I win—tails, you lose. No appeal to facts can affect the preordained conclusion. America is, by tacit definition, oppressive; hence, no significant change is possible within the "system."

The Servitude to Words: Evading the Essential

I cite the cases of McLuhan and Marcuse, both of whom have attracted wide attention in recent years, as evidence of the increasing servitude to words that Gabriel Marcel so feared and deplored. Some may argue that in their cases the defect arose from cloudy rhetoric, and that the remedy is to be found in greater insistence on clarity of language. In part this is true. Yet we should note that blind insistence on linguistic clarity can lead us back into the same thicket and produce its own kind of mental paralysis. Consider, for example, the question of whether it is ever morally justified to punish innocent persons for acts that they did not perform and with which they were in no way connected. Historically, there have been moral theories that permitted this. In the earlier books (chronologically) of the Old Testament, one finds cases where an entire group was made to suffer for a sin committed against God by certain of its members. And the notion of the ancestral curse, passed down from a father to his descendants, is familiar in Greek tragedy. In more modern times it has sometimes been the practice to take hostages for the good behavior of a village and to punish them if their neighbors violated an order. Such theories may be described as theories of *vicarious responsibility*.

Can you dispose of the problem by arguing that the proper definition of the word *punishment* precludes vicarious responsibility, as

A. M. Quinton does? According to him, "The necessity of not punishing the innocent is not moral but logical. It is not that we *may* not punish the innocent and *ought* only to punish the guilty, but that we *cannot* punish the innocent and *must* only punish the guilty. Of course, the suffering or harm in which punishment consists can be and is inflicted on innocent people; but this is not punishment, it is judicial error or terrorism. The infliction of suffering on a person is only properly described as punishment if that person is guilty." Quinton concludes, in short, that the issue does not involve a moral doctrine but rather the proper meaning of the word *punishment*. This way of dealing with the problem is rejected by H. L. A. Hart, theorist of moral law, as "an abuse of definition." Deploring what he calls the method of the *definitional stop*, Hart claims (rightly, in my view) that "no account of punishment can afford to dismiss this question with a definition."

The link between Quinton and Marcuse—who are poles apart in their philosophical stance—is found in their readiness to use definitions of words to foreclose or evade questions that demand serious attention. Quinton does this explicitly in the interest of logical clarity. Marcuse does it implicitly in the interest of political and social reconstruction. But the results are parallel. In both cases the disposition is to fit thought to words rather than to fit words to thought. Thus the packaging takes priority over the contents; the vehicle determines the cargo; the verbal medium restricts the message.

Politics and Language: What is Needed?

The problem is too complex and goes too deep to be soluble by any set of mechanical rules. What is called for is a disposition toward constant self-criticism, coupled with a lively awareness of the dangers of what George Orwell, in his best known book, *1984*, called "newspeak" and "doublethink." It was Orwell's firm conviction that corruption of language leads to corruption of thought, which leads in turn to the corruption of man and society. In 1946 he wrote an essay entitled "Politics and the English Language" in which he discussed the general deterioration of language in our day, with examples drawn from various writers, including some prominent academicians. His main claim was that clear thinking is necessary to intelligent political action and that clear language is necessary to clear thinking.

> Now, it is clear that the decline of a language must ultimately have political and economic causes; it is not due simply to the

bad influence of this or that individual writer. But an effect can become a cause, reinforcing the original cause and producing the same effect in an intensified form, and so on indefinitely. A man may take to drink because he feels himself to be a failure, and then fail all the more completely because he drinks. It is rather the same thing that is happening to the English language. It becomes ugly and inaccurate because our thoughts are foolish, but the slovenliness of our language makes it easier for us to have foolish thoughts. The point is that the process is reversible. Modern English, especially written English, is full of bad habits which spread by imitation and which can be avoided if one is willing to take the necessary first step toward political regeneration.

After observing that "the present political chaos is connected with the decay of language," Orwell goes on to issue a general indictment: "Political language—and with variations this is true of all political parties from Conservatives to Anarchists—is designed to make lies sound truthful and murder respectable, and to give an appearance of solidity to pure wind."

In the twenty-seven years since Orwell wrote his essay, deterioration of language has not lessened; it has increased. And this has occurred on all sides. Charles Frankel of Columbia University blamed the "illusion of words" for Congressional intransigence in foreign policy. This illusion, he said several years ago:

> ... shows itself in a tendency to treat certain words as things in themselves, and to deal with problems by throwing words at them rather than by looking at the facts. . . . The growing conflict between different centers of power within the so-called "Socialist camp" has been plainly visible for some time. . . . Yet Congress, bemused by the phrase "International Communism," chose to act on the assumption that international communism is tightly unified. . . . Such action suggests that the word "Communism" is the enemy, and not the complex phenomenon which the word actually designates. . . .
>
> This free way with words brings a quality of unreality to our public discussions. It leads some people to think we are hysterical and it leads kinder observers to suspect that if we are not hysterical, we are certainly rigid with logophobia.

And in a March 1971 *Time* magazine essay, Melvin Maddocks observes that "with frightening perversity—the evidence mounts daily—words now seem to cut off and isolate, to cause more misunderstandings than they prevent. In the vocabulary of the 1970s, there is adequate language for fanaticism, but none for ordinary quiet conviction. And there are almost no words left to express the concerns of honor, duty, or piety."

There is no need to dwell on the obvious. But it is well to consider the gravity of the situation. Academicians are apt, by force of habit, to regard confused speaking and writing as unfortunate but not necessarily dangerous. The political zealots of the right and left insist that fervor is what counts and that *commitment*—which is usually taken to mean feeling strong emotions—is more important than making clear what one is *committed to*. Meanwhile, the ordinary citizen stops his ears and hopes that the clamor will die away. But I believe we should take to heart what Albert Camus said in *The Rebel* some twenty years ago:

> Every ambiguity, every misunderstanding, leads to death; clear language and simple words are the only salvation from this death. The climax of every tragedy lies in the deafness of its heroes. . . . On the stage as in reality, the monologue precedes death. Every rebel, solely by the movement that sets him in opposition to the oppressor, therefore pleads for life, undertakes to struggle against servitude, falsehood, and terror, and affirms in a flash that these three afflictions are the cause of silence between men, that they obscure them from one another and prevent them from rediscovering themselves in the only value that can save them from nihilism—the long complicity of men at grips with their destiny.

The plain fact is that the systematic deterioration of language in times of crisis prevents dialogue when it is most needed, and thereby contributes to the difficulty of obtaining the kind of concerted action necessary to cope with the mounting complexities of our day. Language, like currency, to which it is often compared, appears to be subject to Gresham's law that debased currency drives out sound coin. What we are now facing is a progressive linguistic inflation that in the long run may turn out to be a more serious threat than the monetary inflation we are experiencing today. Orwell's essay warns us explicitly against pretentious euphemisms, jargon words, and "the inflated style" that "falls upon the facts like soft snow, blurring the outlines and covering up all the details."

When Words Change Their Meanings

We are back, in a sense, to Thucydides' time when "words changed their meanings and were construed in new senses," with disastrous results for communication and mutual understanding. It is worth considering a few specific examples. Some of them show how the uncritical use of metaphors and models can serve not merely to generate ambiguities, but even to give the same word diametrically opposite meanings.

Consider the topic of *relevance* in education, which was much talked about in the late 1960s. There is less talk of relevance today because most people have come to realize that the word has degenerated into an empty slogan. But we would do well to notice that what took place here amounted to a virtual reversal of meaning. In the most familiar sense, education is irrelevant if it is superfluous or if it fails to prepare a student to cope with the real world he enters after graduation. Henry Adams, the distinguished American historian, retrospectively criticized the Harvard education he had received in the 1850s on the ground that it was a waste of time because what he learned had no relation to the practicalities of later life. His college education had been, in effect, aimed at a traditional ideal rather than a current actuality. Fifty or sixty years later that situation had largely changed, and John Dewey, the eminent philosopher who was greatly concerned with education, directed his attention to problems of making education effective as a preparation for membership in a modern democratic and technologically oriented society.

When students in the 1960s raised the cry of "irrelevance," however, they were no longer asserting that education was ineffective in preparing students for their roles in the real world as it currently exists. On the contrary, they meant that it was altogether too effective for that purpose. The burden of their complaint was that the actual state of society is wrong, and that education should be made relevant to their conception of an *ideal society* which should replace the present reality. If one is in sympathy with this position (as I am), one can only deplore the fact that it should have been substantially discredited by clumsy advocacy. By invoking the word *relevance* in a sense opposite to its customary sense, the partisans of educational change clouded the issues beyond hope and made constructive debate impossible. If you are invoking an *ideal model* of man or society, it is essential to specify what ideal model you are invoking. Otherwise, you risk falling into jargon where the words become missiles to throw at problems rather than tools for their clarification.

Another word that has acquired opposite meanings by being applied indiscriminately to actualities and to ideal possibilities is *alienation*. The word alienation has come into vogue in the last two decades, so much so that one may expect to encounter it today in almost any discussion of current problems by political theorists, sociologists, psychologists, educators, philosophers, religious writers, or essayists. The word gained currency first in academic circles and has lately passed into the popular vocabulary. But wide usage has not served to sharpen its meaning. After making a systematic survey, including an historical study, of the origins and manifold modern uses of the term, the philosopher Richard Schacht recently concluded that "it has become a fetish word, and people seem to delight in finding ever different uses for it." On the evidence, this seems to be a modest assessment of the pervasive confusion.

The popularity of this word is due principally, I believe, to the fact that it originally connoted *estrangement*, and estrangement takes so many forms that it can be found one way or another in almost any situation. If writers were content to use the word estrangement, I suspect they would immediately be conscious of its vagueness, but a term like alienation gives an impression of depth and solidity to disarm the critical sense. Sociological writers on the whole have been careful to define what they mean by alienation when they use this term, though their definitions are by no means uniform. But other writers have been less cautious. Many seem to have surrendered to the word (to adopt Orwell's phrase) on the assumption that because it is widely used it must have some central core of essential meaning, and on the further assumption that because it has come into prominence in recent years it must have some special bearing on the present crisis. Those who make these two assumptions usually make a third assumption, too, namely, that alienation is necessarily bad and the immediate task is to find ways to get rid of it.

One such writer is Ernest Becker, who published a book six years ago called *Beyond Alienation: A Philosophy of Education for the Crisis of Democracy*. Becker argues that what we need is a "new moral view of the world," a point with which I would heartily agree. But he goes on to claim that what is needed for this purpose is a "general theory of alienation." If this topic became the central theme of the educational curriculum, and if we could arrive at an adequate theory of alienation, he argues, we should then have the necessary foundation for the "new moral view of the world" that we need to overcome the current crisis. The key notion here is that the word alienation refers to, or expresses, *the* special and central problem of our day. Becker is quite specific about this, asserting that "twentieth-century man is adumbrating his *idea*: alienation. Alienation in modern society. It seems to be the word that characterizes our time, or better, the one that tries to come to grips fumblingly with the problem of man in our time. It seems to be the concept wherewith man is trying to lay hold of the knowledge he needs in order to free himself."

Rejecting suggestions that the concept of alienation may be too loose and vague to be useful, Becker claims that its very breadth of application shows its importance. Another scholar, Bernard Murchland, takes the same view. Murchland, like Becker, treats alienation as something inherently bad and as a peculiar evil of our day. Interestingly, he observes that "language itself has been victimized by alienation," meaning that the practical effectiveness of language as a vehicle of communication has been harmed by certain prevalent philosophical views about the nature of knowledge and personal identity.

Writings of this sort are open to at least three kinds of objection. First, if we take alienation to signify a sense of social discontent and estrangement from reality, it may well be that uncritical talk about alienation is a potent cause of the phenomenon in question. That is, when it is fashionable to be preoccupied with human estrangement, the feeling of estrangement naturally spreads. I have already quoted Leon Eisenberg on the self-fulfilling aspect of popular theories about human nature. This looks like a case in point.

Second, if alienation means estrangement, it does not follow that estrangement is necessarily bad. To Hegel, as F. H. Heinemann has noted, all creativity implied a kind of estrangement, a specific phenomenon, that might be called, in Heinemann's words, "creative alienation." This remark can easily be generalized, I think. Anything really new involves a departure (and so an estrangement) from what has gone before. All creative artists are moved by some sort of discontent. The great critics, reformers, innovators, and revolutionaries of history, in all fields and at all times and places, have been alienated. And so have most of the great heroes of literature. Only someone who believes, consciously or unconsciously, that every individual ought to live a life of total and contented adjustment to society can believe that *all* alienation is bad.

Finally, and perhaps most important, the word alienation has acquired among its many other senses two that are almost opposite, both stemming from the early writings of Marx. It may signify either *maladjustment* or *overadjustment*. In the first sense (which is the one commonly employed today by sociologists) a state of alienation is a condition of felt frustration. The alienated person feels unhappy about society, his neighbors, his career, his family, or the world in general. In the second sense, the alienated person feels perfectly happy but others judge that his happiness is unjustified because he is not achieving what *they* regard as his *ideal* nature. Thus two different kinds of estrangement are involved. In one case, a person is estranged (in some sense) from his *actual* self; in the other, he is estranged from an *ideal* self or an *ideal* possibility of self-realization, with which he may be wholly unconcerned. Both situations are comprehended under the term alienation.

In justice to Marx, it should be noted that he did not, in any of the mature writings published during his lifetime, couch his criticisms of capitalism in terms of alienation; in fact he criticized the word and found other language more suitable to his own purposes. But when his early and previously unpublished manuscripts were brought to light, and especially when the effort was made to *existentialize* Marx on the basis of his early writings, these conflicting senses of alienation were reintroduced to spread confusion.

Another word that has acquired a variety of different meanings, some even involving a reversal of the original meaning, is *revolution.* If we speak of the revolutions of the heavenly bodies, as Copernicus did in his epoch-making work *De Revolutionibus Orbium Coelestium,* we are speaking of a cyclical motion which proceeds smoothly. There is no implication here of disruption, disorder, or discontinuity, but only of regularity and conformity to fixed laws. This sense of revolution, which seems to have been the original sense, is still familiar in the field of mechanics. When the term was first extended metaphorically to the political sphere, it was applied to changes of government which were regarded as reestablishing previous institutional patterns. Thus the peaceful accession of William and Mary to the throne of England in 1688 was called the "glorious revolution," the implication being that it brought about a restoration of former liberties. The idea that a political or economic revolution involves a transition to a new condition of things came later, and involved almost a reversal of meaning.

Futhermore, a change toward radical novelty can take different forms. It can involve a relatively slow and orderly development accomplished peaceably or a sudden dramatic shift marked by violence and disorder. When we speak of the industrial revolution of the late eighteenth and early nineteenth centuries or the technological revolution of today, we are using the term in the former sense. The latter sense of the term seems to have been arrived at by taking the French Revolution, with its dramatic disruptions and bitter civil disorders, as a controlling model or paradigm of "revolutionary" change.

One effect of Marx's writings was to identify the concept of social revolution with an abrupt and cataclysmic struggle in which an existing social order is violently overturned by a rebellious exploited class. Two aspects of his usage should be stressed. First, there arises a sharp distinction between revolution and reform—a distinction that does not arise when the word revolution is used in any of its other senses. Second, social revolution, in the Marxian context, is viewed as a part of the historical process; revolution may be abrupt, violent, and traumatic, but it does not involve a total break with the past. For a classical Marxist, there is no such thing as historical discontinuity. Rather the revolt of the proletariat, which is seen as leading to the establishment of the classless society, is also seen as growing directly and necessarily from the tensions generated within capitalistic society.

I make this point because some writers of the New Left have talked of revolution as if it were a means of obliterating history, or at least of creating a total discontinuity between past and future. Because present society is evil, it must be totally destroyed so that a new society may be rebuilt from a fresh base. Here the mission of the revolutionary is seen as purely negative; he is not moved by hopes of building a better future for mankind, but by a consuming personal hatred for present evil. Let me quote from Carl Oglesby, a spokesman for the New Left: "The fundamental revolutionary motive is not to construct a Paradise but to destroy an Inferno. . . . It cannot be too much emphasized that the interest in developing other social forms, however acute it may become, follows, *does not precede*, the soul-basic explosion against injustice which is the one redemption of the damned."

Here the word revolutionary has lost all connection with its origins. It would be more intelligible and more honest in this context to speak of simple destruction rather than of revolution. But rhetoric has taken over, and the writer has been victimized by words. If it be claimed that there is in the background a new ideal model of revolutionary change— a model that suggests we must first tear down existing social institutions before we can set about building new ones—the answer is that the metaphor is incomplete. When you knock down a building, you are not left with a clean site, but with a pile of rubble on which nothing whatever can be constructed.

As should be plain at this point, there is no clear foundation for the common assumption that there is a fundamental and ultimate distinction between revolution and reform. This distinction is artificial and depends upon the selection of one particular model of revolutionary change over other models that have at least equal claim to recognition. What is needed is a careful reexamination of the whole concept of revolution in light of its manifest ambiguity. This was a central argument of the French writer Jean-François Revel in his recent book, *Without Marx or Jesus*. This argument has been strongly resisted by those who, being wedded to a particular verbal orthodoxy, assume that revolution and reform must be antithetical simply because *they* have grown accustomed to making the distinction. Here again, thought is in servitude to words.

Abstractions Grounded in the Air

As overextension of a particular model can create a delusive appearance of clarity, confusion can also result when appropriate models are ignored or—which often comes to the same thing—when no consideration is given to the application of general terms to concrete actualities. An example is afforded by Prof. George W. Morgan's book *The Human Predicament: Dissolution and Wholeness*, published in 1968. Professor Morgan rejects (as I do) the philosophical position of Hans Reichenbach and Bertrand Russell. But he does so largely by piling up broad generalizations without attention to their specific applications and by applying verbal labels without concern for their implications. Morgan explicitly condemns undue reliance on abstractions—and then does the very thing he condemns.

As to the nature of human *wholeness*, Morgan makes a series of statements like these:

> By *whole* I mean unreduced and undivided. The man who is whole acknowledges and unifies all elements of his human self. . . . Wholeness means that the diverse resources of the self and diverse attitudes toward the world are not merely present side by side but are unified. It means that every activity is shaped by the whole self. . . . A person is not free to be in the world unless every part of him is potentially present at every moment of life. . . . Only if all the elements of the self can be called upon in every occasion is self-government possible.

Since he gives no examples, he apparently thinks that these statements are clear. The trouble is that, as there are different kinds of wholes and different types of part-whole relations, there are different senses of the words *whole* and *wholeness*. With respect to an object like a dinner plate, we might say that to be whole is to be undivided and unbroken. With respect to a machine like an engine, we might say that to be whole is to have all parts functioning together in unison. Morgan's view of wholeness seems to fit objects of these sorts. But as applied to human beings, the words *whole* and *wholeness* have a different import: they imply soundness, health, freedom from incapacity or disability. To understand wholeness in this sense, it is necessary to consider specific models of human character (actual or ideal) as has been done by psychologists such as Gordon Allport, Erik Erikson, or Abraham Maslow, who have worked to clarify the difficult concepts of human identity and human personality. Presumably a "whole" person eats, sleeps, makes love, thinks, reads, writes, appreciates art, etc. But nobody can perform all such activities at the same time. Indeed, most human capacities are specialized so that the effective exercise of one requires the temporary suspension of others. As applied to actual individuals, Morgan's vague generalizations are more mystifying than helpful. If he had stopped to consider concrete cases, if he had looked at the ongoing work of psychologists or personality theorists, or if he had tried to put forward some ideal model of human wholeness as he conceives it, he would surely have seen the difficulty. Instead, he has let the tide of words sweep him along. The results are paradoxical. He strongly rejects the idea that men should be treated as machines, yet he himself treats human wholeness as if it were mechanical wholeness.

Morgan further claims that the chief enemy of human wholeness today is what he calls the "prosaic mentality." It turns out that the prosaic mentality, as he describes it, is identical with the philosophical outlook of Bertrand Russell. Now I believe, as I have said, that Lord Russell's philosophical views are mistaken. But surely nobody in his right mind could suggest that Russell was *prosaic*. Yet such is the necessary implication of Morgan's description—if it is taken seriously.

Let me add that Morgan's book is by no means an extreme example. It is rather more thoughtful than many books of its type and it has been commended by several prominent writers. The fact remains that it exhibits the same servitude to words which Marcel deplored—the same deterioration of language against which Orwell protested. In my judgment it does more damage to the humanist position than to the views which Morgan wishes to attack. It confuses vital issues almost beyond hope of clarification.

We must recall, of course, that De Tocqueville many years ago noted the fondness of Americans for loose abstractions, observing that "an abstract term is like a box with a false bottom: you may put in it what ideas you please, and take them out again without being observed." What is alarming is that the habit has now spread to those whose supposed function is to encourage clarity and intellectual honesty in the interests of effective communication and debate. We have come to accept without objection novel terms like *racism* and *sexism* which, because of their very vagueness, function as epithets rather than as intelligible descriptions. I believe that we should avoid false-bottom words and direct our attention to the concrete phenomena which call for concrete remedies.

CHAPTER FOUR

CLASSICAL VIEWS OF MAN

THE MEDIEVAL THEOLOGIANS had no such uncertainty about the nature of man as troubles us today. For them, man was the central figure in the cosmic drama, not because of his own merits, but because of God's concern for him. In this context, the whole of natural creation was seen as a great stage on which the drama of human salvation was played out, the stage itself having been created for the sake of the play. In the Judeo-Christian tradition man was the product of a special act of Divine creation, but so was the rest of the natural universe. God's creative act did not set man apart from nature, but set him centrally and immediately within it, occupying a middle point in the hierarchy of being, above inanimate objects and other living creatures of earth but below the angels. The idea of a special creation has now virtually disappeared, and with it the idea of a divinely ordered hierarchy of being. Today man is seen to have emerged in the process of natural evolution and to have reached his present position of power and authority by virtue of his natural capacities, there to stand—for better or worse—on his own two feet.

The difficulty of forming a clear conception of man's nature is that one cannot isolate it for examination. The creature we call man always appears within an environmental context, including a cultural context, by which he is conditioned. And environment and culture vary.

As Aristotle quite rightly said, a being who can live in isolation from society must be either a beast or a god. Man is, in short, a *social* animay; to abstract him from society and culture is impossible. Yet, man owes much to his genetic inheritance, without which he could neither act as he does in his social context nor be subject, as he obviously is, to the influences of social conditioning and learning.

I am not interested here in entering the debate over the relative weight of the genetic component as opposed to the cultural component in man's behavior. When I speak of human nature I am concerned with what emerges from the interaction of both factors. In other words, I am interested in patterns of behavior exhibited by concrete individuals, each possessing a unique combination of genes and standing as the product of different cultures or subcultures.

Are useful generalizations possible where such diversity exists? I believe they are. As I have said, history is one of our best sources of information about man, and especially about the workings of the human mind. More than that, the mere fact that we can in some measure understand and imaginatively reproduce, however incompletely, the outlooks, attitudes, and actions of men from other times and places in contexts very different from our own is strong evidence that there is some common core of human experience. And if we find that despite wide cultural variation (and individual genetic variation) there are recurrent and persistent problems which have forced themselves on the attention of thinking men in all ages of recorded history, we may be reasonably confident that such problems are fundamental to the human condition, and that men's efforts to wrestle with them throw light on certain important aspects of the human mind.

Plato and Aristotle: Philosophy Begins in Wonder

In our search for the meaning of man, then, let us go back through history to the time of the great Greek philosophers. For Plato and Aristotle, philosophy began in *wonder*—a word that meant a blend of curiosity and amazement. They had, in Whitehead's phrase, "the genius to be astonished." Now astonishment or amazement can sometimes inhibit inquiry, as in the case of Job, who was reduced to reverent and receptive silence by the majesty and power of God's discourse to him out of the whirlwind. But amazement can also stimulate inquiry if it is coupled with curiosity—not idle curiosity or even the kind of intellectual itchiness or rational disquietude we speak of today as "intellectual curiosity," but an attentive beholding leading to an appreciative comprehension.

"All men by nature desire to know," Aristotle wrote in the opening passage of his *Metaphysics*. The quest for knowledge was for him, as for Plato, a quest for understanding, colored always by the sense of wonder and delight. For that reason, *theoria*—which meant something very different from what we mean today by the phrase "theoretical knowledge"—signified rapt contemplation of those fundamental principles of reality that, precisely because they are fundamental, cannot be modified by any human action but can only be contemplated. Moreover, Plato and Aristotle believed that man achieved his most abiding satisfaction and the fullest realization of his distinctively human potentialities in the delighted contemplation of the ultimate principles of reality. This idea was carried over into medieval theology and is reflected in the concept of the beatific vision of God, as poetically portrayed in Dante's *Paradiso*.

Two points require special emphasis before proceeding further. One is that conceptions of the nature and function of human knowledge are naturally and necessarily correlated with conceptions of the nature of man. If man is conceived as a distinctively *rational* animal and *reason* as a natural capacity for understanding, the acquistion of understanding will naturally stand as the highest goal of human striving and the most perfect realization of human capacities. In this light, *theoria*, or knowledge, is quite literally its own reward, since there is no higher satisfaction possible for any man. A perceptive discussion of the great differences between the Aristotelian and Thomistic conceptions of *theory*, on the one hand, and the Baconian and post-Baconian conceptions of theory on the other, is to be found in an essay by Hans Jonas on "The Practical Uses of Theory," in his book *The Phenomenon of Life*. Jonas correctly points out that once it came to be believed that knowledge is to be sought for the benefit of humanity, and not (primarily) for the ennoblement and satisfaction of the knower, the conception of *theoretical knowledge* was radically altered—along with the underlying conception of human nature itself. This individualistic element implicit in the Aristotelian and Thomistic conception has not always been appreciated.

The second point I want to emphasize has to do with the visual or optical model of knowledge. I spoke earlier of the pervasive influence of metaphors and models on all our thinking, and suggested that our effort should not be to eliminate them—which even if it were possible would seriously impair our ability to deal with new situations—but simply to become aware of their existence in order to appreciate their several strengths and weaknesses. It is clear that the visual model of knowledge was already embedded early in the language of the Greeks.

It is equally clear that the visual model of knowledge does *not* imply the emotional detachment or disengagement of the knower from the object known. When we see something with our eyes, we do not stand in an emotional vacuum. We may see an object or a person with surprise, anger, fear, relief, joy, interest, solicitude, affection, amusement, boredom, or fascinated concern. Whatever the case, every instance of seeing, like every instance of perception by the other senses, occurs within a context of feeling and emotion. The same is true of knowing. There is no such thing as simply knowing, or simply being aware, without an accompanying attitude. Plato and Aristotle knew this.

Feeling and Knowing

One of the most curious, and most artificial, aspects of modern value theory is its attempt to separate "cognitive" interests from all other human interests and attitudes, as if they could occur in disjunction. The fact is that we never feel attracted to or repelled by anything without some kind of cognitive awareness of it; nor can we be aware of anything without having an attitude toward it, if only casual indifference. To separate knowing from feeling is possible conceptually, but to project this conceptual distinction onto concrete experience is to commit what Whitehead calls the fallacy of misplaced concreteness—that is, it involves mistaking an abstraction of thought for concrete reality. The truth is that all items encountered in experience are suffused with emotional color. We may choose to disregard such emotional color for certain purposes and to damp down our emotional reactions, lest they distract attention from more important aspects of the data at hand. But the idea of a "sheer" fact or a "mere" fact as simply presented to our awareness without emotional overtones is, as Whitehead insists, an abstract mental construction. It originates, I believe, from the old model of mind as *tabula rasa*, a blank tablet or sheet of empty paper, on which experience writes. Locke and other empiricists employed this model as a step in getting rid of the "rationalist" belief in innate ideas. Yet the model has serious weaknesses of its own, for the mind is in fact never a blank (at least after the first days of infant life). Rather it is a developing system of activities, habits, and associations in which new experiences are not merely added to old ones, like goods being accumulated in a warehouse, but are worked into developing patterns of significance. All data occur within a context, a context which necessarily includes on the side of the recipient an elaborate network of concepts, models, and associations which are normative in function and pervaded by feeling and emotion.

I have said that Plato and Aristotle did not separate knowing from feeling. But neither did they separate knowing from acting or making. They clearly recognized that man is an animal who knows, feels, acts, and makes new things. But because they believed that both acting and making if properly conducted depend (in some sense) on knowing (in some form), they gave primacy to knowing as the distinctive and primary capacity of man. This rationalistic or intellectualistic view of man is altogether foreign to modern conceptions, which generally give primacy to feeling, acting, or innovative making. Still, we should note that Plato and Aristotle were not typical of Greek thought in general (great philosophers are never typical of their ages), and that there were other important strains of Greek thinking. By contrasting them with the Platonic and Aristotelian conception, we may be able to cast light on several recurrent issues.

The Greek Tragedians

There is a notable passage in Aeschylus' *Prometheus Bound* in which man's capacity for technological invention is seen as his primary resource. It is one of the earliest passages in Western literature in which the process of cultural evolution is described. Man's inventiveness is seen as a divine dispensation, the gift of Prometheus, who was made to suffer for this kindness to man by Zeus, here portrayed (most untypically) as a malevolent deity unfriendly to man. The passage in question, which runs for more than sixty lines, is too long to quote in full, but it covers almost the whole range of early technological achievement. It includes not only the use of fire, the building of shelters, the domestication of animals, the working of metals, and the introduction of agriculture, medicine, and navigation, but also the use of language, mathematics, astronomy, and the arts of divination. All these are treated as fruits of intelligence. The passage in Edith Hamilton's rendering begins with Prometheus saying:

> Hear rather all that mortals suffered.
> Once they were fools. I gave them power to think.
> Through me they won their minds. . . .
> Seeing they did not see nor hearing hear.
> Like dreams they led a random life.

The long catalogue of the fruits of man's inventiveness concludes with the statement, "All arts, all goods, have come to men from me." The governing term here is *technai*, the plural form of the word *techné*, from which we derive the words technique, technical, and of course technology. The root meaning signifies skill or art in doing something or making something. Man is conceived as a technically gifted animal whose mental powers are exhibited primarily in his active ingenuity.

But inventiveness is obviously double-faced. One who does new things and makes new devices soon finds that such activities can get him into trouble. The Greek fable of Icarus makes the point. When Daedalus, the cunning inventor, manufactured wings out of feathers and wax and gave a pair to his son Icarus, he warned Icarus not to fly so low that the wings would be wetted by the sea or so high that the wax would be melted by the sun. But Icarus, intoxicated by the joy of flight, flew high and so fell to his death. The parable is clear: technological innovation can be destructive.

The same holds true for human action. All the Greek tragedians appreciated the dilemma of moral conflicts, especially those involving a collision not between right and wrong but rather between right and right. Sophocles' *Oedipus Rex* is built around the idea that even well-intended acts can be self-defeating when the true situation is not rightly understood. Man himself, when looked at critically, is thus seen as an amazing, even frightening object, because of the ambivalent aspects of his powers of doing and making. In Sophocles' famous choral ode in *Antigone*, the adjective *deinos*, signifying something strange, wonderful, and terrifying, is applied to man. There are many wondrous things in the world, the Chorus sings, but none more amazing and terrifying than man himself, whose extraordinary powers can produce both unprecedented good and unprecedented evil. The Greek poets, notably Euripides, were of course also conscious of the force of passion and the demonic power of human emotions when deeply stirred.

Man's Over-reaching Pride: "Hybris"

It was evidently from this awareness of the ambivalence of human powers that all the Greeks came to associate wisdom with balance and moderation, a concept, as we have seen, quite different from the modern view of moderation. It was in the same context that there developed the Greek view of *hybris*, a word that we customarily translate as pride. But our word has somewhat different connotations: for us, the opposite of pride is humility; whereas for the Greeks the opposite of *hybris* was sound judgment with a clear estimate of the ambiguities of the human situation and the ambivalence of human capacities.

In the third choric song of Sophocles' *Oedipus Rex*, the first antistrophe begins with the words *"Hybris phyteui tyrannon / Hybris...."*

The verb is clear enough: it means to breed or engender—a common literal rendering of the passage being "Insolence begets the tyrant," or "Of insolence is bred the tyrant." But Kenneth Cavander, departing from the literal rendering, comes closer, I believe, to the intended significance with "Yet man desires to be more than man, to rule / His world for himself." *Hybris* is an expression of man's impulse to become "more than man" and the word *tyrannon* here signifies, not despotic political rule (clearly, Oedipus ruled Thebes well), but something broader; namely, inappropriate power that goes beyond due limits. As the same choric ode goes on to assert a few lines later, *hybris* may sometimes work for the public good, in which case it is to be applauded rather than condemned. So human *hybris* is itself ambivalent. Man may have to go beyond the boundaries of his proper condition to discover where the limits are. Even then, the limits may remain indefinite. Man explores, but does so at his peril.

In the Judeo-Christian tradition there is, of course, a similar insistence that man must keep his proper place, walking humbly before God and avoiding the sin of pride, which would breach this obligation. But in this tradition, man's proper place was thought to have been clearly marked out for him by the specific prescriptions of God's laws. Hence, one source of ambiguity was removed. In the Greek context man was seen as a part of nature, with an extraordinary role to play because of his unusual powers, but it was left to man himself to discover the nature of his special role and its limitations. Whereas in *Prometheus Bound* Aeschylus celebrated the great intellectual powers of man, most other Greek tragedies (including the bulk of those written by Aeschylus himself) were concerned with the miscarriages of power.

In brief, the Greeks were aware of the truth of Lord Acton's maxim that power tends to corrupt those who exercise it. They saw this principle as applying to all types of human power, including technological inventiveness. If we could imagine a thinker from classical Greece looking at our modern industrial world, we might expect him to say, "Your blind faith in man's capacity for unlimited progress and growth through technological expansion is a form of *hybris*, necessarily inviting disaster. It is not evil *per se*. The evil comes from the same over-confidence and disregard for natural limits that have always been man's weaknesses. For this the only remedy is *wisdom*."

Understanding and Action

Jonas and others have argued plausibly that the search for truth is prompted by the experience of error, which I interpret broadly to cover the generalized feeling that things are not acceptable as they stand. In its more customary sense, the word *error* is opposed to truth; hence to speak of error is to presuppose the existence of truth. But in a broader sense, to err is simply to stray. I would argue, contrary to the views of Plato and Aristotle, that searching for truth is not an effort to *discover* something already there (like searching for gold hidden in the earth); but rather an effort (often involving conceptual readjustment) to set up criteria for assessing the reliability or trustworthiness of ideas and beliefs. In this context the sense of error is the sense that one lacks such criteria; it does not imply that such criteria exist awaiting discovery, but that man must invent them.

However this may be, it seems apparent that the views of Plato and Aristotle arose as a reaction against a widespread tide of anti-intellectualism.

Plato was born in the early years of the Peloponnesian War and grew up to see its disastrous consequences on Athens. The demoralization of Athenian democracy was exemplified by the execution of Socrates in 399 B.C. while Plato was still a young man. Plato's intellectualism was not an escape from reality, but was intended as a very practical attempt to confront the chaos of the times and to bring order out of it. Moral and political action was of major concern to both Plato and Aristotle, and though they differed as to the nature of the relation between knowing and acting, they agreed that effective action requires some kind of knowing and understanding. Each had something to say about the inventiveness of the artist and the poet, though I think a modern reader would have to say that they unjustly devalued human inventiveness, notably technological inventiveness. But their abiding legacy was their conviction that *the need for intellectual understanding is fundamental to man and that in the end effective human action depends upon it.*

CHAPTER FIVE

MODERN VIEWS OF MAN: VOLUNTARISM

ONE OF THE GREAT problems with which any rationalist or intellectualist view of man has to wrestle is the connection between knowing and choosing. It is one thing to assert generally that reason determines (or should determine) the making of decisions, but it is something else to explain how knowledge gets translated into action. Despite suggestions in Plato's early Socratic dialogues that if a man knows what is good, he will automatically do it (which seems to imply that all wrong action is due to some kind of intellectual mistake), later thinkers, beginning with Aristotle, have recognized that it is possible for a man to know what is right but not to do it. As St. Paul put it, we see the better course but follow the worse.

According to theological *voluntarism*, God's will is absolute and subject to no limitations. This view was maintained by William of Ockham in opposition to Thomas Aquinas. Aquinas held that God's will is limited by His own nature; therefore, God can will neither a contradiction nor any evil. In such a view (which is in the spirit of Plato and Aristotle), God forbids murder because murder is wrong; it is not made wrong simply because God forbids it. Ockham took the other view, holding that God's will is unlimited in any respect and is itself the ultimate basis of right and wrong. The difference may seem subtle and technical, but in fact it is momentous, especially when transferred to the human level. All so-called natural-law theories proceed on the assumption that certain acts or dispositions of character are inherently right and others inherently wrong, and that man, by using his reason or his conscience, can learn what these are. Voluntarism denies this, asserting in effect that right and wrong are established only by the command or decree of some authority—God, a human monarch, a legislature, etc. In this view it makes no sense to ask whether God's will is righteous, because by definition whatever God wills is right. Similarly, on a secular level, the king can do no wrong because the king's decree is the basis of right. The result of such a view is that there is no right or wrong except by *fiat*. This is the position taken in modern days by legal positivism, which holds that the positive law of any society, if duly enacted by the appropriate authority, is for that society the measure of right and wrong.

Free Choice

Modern existentialism has plausibly been seen as an individualistic form of voluntarism (notably by Frederick Olafson in his book *Principles and Persons*). The stress here is on personal choice; reason is devalued. In the face of God, Kierkegaard's "knight of faith" can only choose to obey God's command, even if (as for Abraham) it means committing an act of murder. If there is no God, then one's own *authentic choice* is both the ground and the measure of what is right. Right and wrong issue from someone's fiat, and for the authentic individual who makes his own free choices there is no legitimate fiat but his own.

I do not mean to suggest that this sort of existentialism sprang direct from the theological voluntarism of Ockham. There were many intermediate stages which, whether or not they establish historical influence, exhibit a generally consistent pattern. Rousseau, for example, in his *Second Discourse*, linked human understanding largely to the passions and selected the capacity to make free choices as the distinctive mark of humans. The distinctive capacity of man is "the power of willing, or rather of choosing."

In this view, which has proved widely influential, the ultimate good of the individual is freedom and autonomy. Observe that Rousseau did not deny that man has a determinate "nature." On the contrary, he asserted that man is by nature good, or at least not evil, and becomes vicious because of social oppression and injustice. Hence, because society itself is the prime cause of evil, to remove this evil society must be reconstructed.

The Perfectibility of Man

Three points deserve special notice before we proceed further. The first is that there was a mounting tide of objection in the eighteenth century to the Christian doctrine of original sin, which by then was considered demeaning to man. There was also a spreading confidence in the perfectibility of man through his own efforts, a confidence that spread in large measure (as we can see in retrospect) because of the dramatic expansions which were in progress on all fronts—geographical, economic, scientific, and technological. Rousseau asserted his belief in man's "capacity for self-perfection" as a distinctive human quality, second in importance only to his faculty of will and choice. He wished to apply this capacity to the matter of political and social reconstruction.

Squaring a Circle: Rousseau's "General Will"

Second, Rousseau did not believe that society could be done away with. He recognized that man is a social animal who cannot exist in isolation. The practical problem, therefore, is to reconstruct society in such a way that the individual within it can achieve his natural capacities for personal autonomy. Rousseau recognized the difficulty clearly enough, observing that "the subjecting of man to law is a problem in politics which I liken to that of the squaring of the circle in geometry." His own effort to square the circle, as put forward in *The Social Contract*, rested on the concept of the *general will*, a universal, collective will which is always directed for the common good—a will which each individual would freely share if he could transcend his own self-interest to know what is good for all. Rousseau sets this concept in contrast to the *will of all*. "There is often a great deal of difference between the *will of all* and the *general will*; the latter takes account only of the common interest, while the former takes private interest into account and is no more than a sum of particular wills." In the ideal society, the individual subjects himself entirely to the general will, reserving no right of protest or disobedience. His individual autonomy is maintained because, in participating in the general will, he is in fact imposing laws upon himself; or as Rousseau states, "Each man, by uniting himself with all others, nevertheless obeys only himself and remains as free as before." Rousseau's theory of the general will has been a subject of considerable debate because it seems to introduce into his political theory a collectivist aspect apparently at odds with his dominantly individualistic position. Without going into this debate, it is fair to say that there are two sides to Rousseau, not altogether easy to reconcile. The individualistic side has had the greater influence, I think, coupled with the view that society itself converts naturally good men into frustrated and vicious men. In the modern idiom, society and social institutions cause the alienation of man.

Man in Nature vs. Man in Society

Third, Rousseau relied heavily upon an old distinction, which goes back to the Greek philosophers, between *nature* and *convention*. For Rousseau, what is natural is sound, reliable, and good; what is conventional is artificial, unreliable, and bad. He saw the laws and conventions of society—at least of all existing civilized societies—as artificial and therefore unnatural.

But there are two major difficulties with this conclusion. First, if man is indeed by nature a social animal, then society must also be a natural development; and if the establishment of norms and conventions is necessary to social cooperation—as is clearly the case—the existence of social conventions cannot be unnatural *per se*. Rousseau seems here to have uncritically taken over the intellectualist preference (reflected in Plato) for what is discovered ready-made over what is man-made. In the second place, it is apparent from the history of thought that the distinction between nature and convention can be used in opposite ways. When nature is viewed as hostile, "red in tooth and claw," one looks to human convention for protection. Thus in *Prometheus Bound* man's inventive powers are seen as his best resource against the forces of an unfriendly universe. Conversely, when social practices or institutions are viewed as hostile, one looks back to nature for the desired model. So the appeal can be made in either direction, according to circumstances.

How these and other difficulties can generate confusion, especially if they are overlooked, can be illustrated by referring to two of the writers mentioned in Chapter Three, both of whom invoke Rousseau. Ernest Becker, who asserts the need for a "new moral view of the world," claims to find the basis for it in "the great Rousseau's truth," which is that "man is *good*." Becker summarizes the point this way: "Man is good; but society renders him evil. This was Rousseau's world-historical message. This proposition is at the same time the *single unifying principle* for our whole curriculum." I suppose that the problems just mentioned in connection with Rousseau's position would find a place in Becker's new curriculum. But another question arises that I have not yet mentioned: if man is good, how has he managed so consistently to create bad societies? (We must remember that Rousseau was not talking about modern industrial technology but about eighteenth-century France.) This leads in turn to another question: to whom does the abstract noun *man* refer in this context? Are we to say that *man* refers not to all men but only to some of them? If so, it seems false and misleading to say that man is good. If some men, though but few, are naturally evil, and if it is they who create repressive institutions, then it is those men (not society as such) who are responsible. If, on the other hand, *man* refers to all men—or all normal men—and if their goodness is to be judged by what they typically produce, then we are forced to conclude that since men regularly produce evil societies, they must themselves be evil to some degree. The fact is, I think, that there is always an interaction between the men who live in a society and the society itself, and such interactions take many forms. Undoubtedly, some men are made evil and aggressive by social influences, but just as certainly other men—having the power of independent choice on which Rousseau insists—are able to resist, and still others may work to reconstruct the society.

Bernard Murchland, author of *The Age of Alienation*, also relies on Rousseau. He asserts (correctly) that Rousseau's picture of natural man was an ideal model. But Murchland proceeds to treat *natural* man as the authentic man and *social* man as an artificial perversion. He fully adopts Rousseau's claim that when man submits to natural constraints (those imposed by physical nature) his submission is morally right, but when he submits to artificial restraints (those imposed by society) he is morally wrong: "Rousseau makes a fundamental distinction. . . . We can be dependent upon things (i.e., circumstances which are decreed by nature) or upon men (the artificial conventions of society and the opinion of others). The first kind of dependence is in perfect conformity with freedom and morality. The second is not. It is rather the source of all immorality." I think Murchland correctly represents Rousseau here. But this supposedly fundamental distinction is patently artificial for the reasons already given. Also, it gives rise to a curiously limited conception of freedom. One of Whitehead's observations on freedom is especially pertinent:

> When we think of freedom, we are apt to confine ourselves to freedom of thought, freedom of the press, freedom of religious opinions. *Then the limitations to freedom are conceived as wholly arising from the antagonisms of our fellow men. This is a thorough mistake.* The massive habits of physical nature, its iron laws, determine the scene for the sufferings of men. Birth and death, heat, cold, hunger, separation, disease,

the general impracticability of purpose, all bring their quota
to imprison the souls of women and of men. . . . *The essence
of freedom is the practicability of purpose.* (Italics added.)

If man is by nature a social animal who cannot live outside society,
and if social living necessitates some degree of cooperation and conformity to accepted practices, how can such conformity be condemned
as intrinsically artificial? Obviously it cannot. Among the most notable
conformists to social customs were the very primitives from whom
Rousseau claimed to have derived his model of natural man. The fact
is that non-conformity is a modern ideal, born in modern societies.
It had no place in tribal societies.

What is also overlooked is that one effect of a developing technology
is always and necessarily to reduce man's subjection to natural forces at
the cost of increased subjection to social pressures and social institutions. Under natural conditions (assuming that the use of draft animals
was "natural," although unknown to some undeveloped societies) it
took months of hazardous travel to move from New England to California. Today the journey may be accomplished, with far less risk, in a
matter of hours. There is far greater freedom of individual movement
today, but at the cost of a vast number of bureaucratic regulations and
of conformity to a great number of prescribed procedures. Whether
there is a net gain or loss to the freedom of the individual depends on
balancing the two sides of the account. The ancient Greeks knew this,
as does anyone who is concerned with concrete actualities rather than
verbal abstractions.

Freedom and Autonomy

I would like to conclude this sketch of the voluntarist conception of
man with a word about autonomy. Can the highest form of human
self-realization possibly consist in the enjoyment of pure autonomy?
Can we believe that autonomy stands as an end in itself? I find this conception hard to take seriously. Freedom, it seems to me, is like money;
its value depends on what you do with it. The miser never enjoys his
hoarded money except by gloating over it. Similarly, the man who
hoards his freedom makes it useless. He can make no commitments,
since any serious commitment limits his subsequent freedom of action.
If autonomy were to be valued as an end in itself—which I think it never
is—it would commit one to a wholly negative existence. Furthermore,
complete autonomy is obviously impossible. The strongest forces conditioning any individual are clearly his genetic inheritance and his early

upbringing. But nobody could ever hope to decide for himself whether to be born, when, to what parents, or in which society. These are matters that depend on the actions and decisions of others, and there is no conceivable way to alter this situation. That the individual is thrown into the world without his consent and under circumstances over which he has no control is a fact of human existence that no social restructuring or technical advance could ever hope to change. Some existentialist and post-existentialist writers rail against this fact as one manifestation of the general "absurdity" of the human condition. But such claims are empty. They reflect the kind of anti-intellectualism which springs from over-intellectualizing, coupled with self-pity and a love for self-dramatization. Dostoevsky's *Underground Man* is the prototype of this kind of thinking. A man who genuinely believes that all human existence is absurd must perforce regard himself and his own disquietudes as also absurd, a realization which immediately breaks the spell. When people assert that human existence is absurd, what they usually seem to mean is: "All existence is absurd, except mine, and I am tragic because I feel the absurdity of everything else."

The desire for freedom and autonomy need not, of course, be pushed to such extremes. Most people believe in freedom within the limits of practical possibility, which still allows for major questions about the limits and where they are. For present purposes, the central issue is whether freedom and autonomy are to be valued as ends in themselves or as means to further ends. Most people take the latter view—as did Plato and Aristotle. Those I have called voluntarists tend to take the former view, treating man's power of will and choice as the basic characteristic of man, and treating autonomy as the final realization of man's nature. Not many people have pushed the voluntarist view to this final limit. Rousseau, for example, did not. As I have tried to suggest, the voluntarist strain in Rousseau is joined (somewhat uneasily) with several others. But some modern writers, especially among the existentialists, have come close to pushing the voluntarist view to its ultimate limit. At that limit the central human reality is the fact that man *chooses*. If man has a nature, it is not pre-given or predetermined. Each individual makes his own character by means of his choices. This is seen as a universal characteristic of the human condition. The existence of human nature is thus pushed out the door only to come back by the window. It is the nature of man to make and remake himself by his free acts of choice. And *authentic* choice in this view is wholly free. But if there are no criteria to guide our choices—if there are no criteria even for distinguishing *authentic* choices from *inauthentic* choices— such freedom is empty. It is a burden rather than a benefit.

CHAPTER SIX

MODERN VIEWS OF MAN: DETERMINISM AND MATERIALISM

DETERMINIST VIEWS OF MAN, far from treating choice as the distinctive capacity of the human being, reject the concept of freedom and choice entirely. Indeed, most such views deny the independence of intellect as well as will, attributing all types of thinking, acting, and making to the interplay between basic psychic structures or drives on one side and environmental pressures or stimulations on the other. The relative weight given to these interacting forces can vary greatly. The behaviorists, for instance, interpret behavior wholly in terms of the organism's responses to environmental stimuli. This emphasis leads readily (though not necessarily, in my opinion) to a mechanistic model of man, according to which man lacks creativity, spontaneity, or purpose and merely reacts to stimuli in ways that are (theoretically) ordered and predictable. The Freudians, in contrast, insist on the primary importance of psychic structures and unconscious motivations, though they also give great weight to the impact of environmental influences during infancy.

Freud: Man as Driven

Still, the status of individual freedom is not wholly clear in Freud. One of his greatest contributions was to create a new image of man, in Rollo May's words, "of man as determined—not *driving* any more, but *driven.*" As Freud saw it, the deeply rooted belief in psychic freedom and choice is unscientific and has to give ground to the claims of a determinism which governs mental life. Yet, as May points out, a paradox arises, for psychoanalytic therapy depends on encouraging the patient to make choices about his own attitudes. May quotes Freud's own statement in *The Ego and the Id* that "analysis does not set out to make pathological reactions impossible, but to give the patient's ego freedom to choose one way or the other." In brief, Freud's theory denies human freedom, but his practice encourages the patient to help himself. Thus, the self is determined; yet in dealing with its own tensions, it must exhibit some degree of self-determination.

The fact remains that the dominant image spread abroad by Freud was that the individual is determined; not driving, but driven. The impact of this image—converging with images drawn from other types of deterministic theories—was inevitably to propagate a sense of individual powerlessness and passivity, undermining the sense of responsibility. It seems clear that Freud's view contributed significantly to the ideal of adjustment, which became pervasive in America in the late 1940s and early 1950s, and which has since been characterized as apathy. According to Freud, the psychic structure of man is such that tension and conflict between the individual and society is inevitable. This was the main theme of his essay *Civilization and Its Discontents.* In this view, although some types of social or political reform might reduce individual repressions, no social restructuring could possibly serve to eliminate them. Ultimately, the individual must come to terms with society by adjusting himself to it, and the mission of therapy is to assist in the process. There emerges what Philip Rieff has called the model of "psychological man" or "therapeutic man." Morally, the emphasis here is placed on honesty, especially honesty in facing and accepting the realities of the human situation and the impossibility of escaping from the conflicts and tensions intrinsic to the human condition. Despite Freud's hostility to religion, it has been noted that his view of man bears some similarity to the Christian view of original sin. In both cases, man is seen as being subject, by genetic inheritance, to tension and conflict; his nature is not in any fundamental sense malleable or perfectible.

Although Freud himself put his faith in science and scientific inquiry, his theories concerning the psyche and its motivations put the grounds of scientific curiosity in doubt. Thus D. C. McClelland, a contemporary writer of evident Freudian background, has felt it necessary to account for the intellectual curiosity of the scientist in terms of some deeper drive, related to either sex or aggression. The quest for intellectual understanding is not here denied. But it no longer stands (as with Aristotle) as the exercise of a basic, natural drive, but instead is a form of secondary activity, engaged in for the sake of working off libidinal or aggressive tensions. Presumably other forms of activity might have served equally well. Here scientific theory seems to reduce the human importance of scientific theorizing.

Skinner: Man as Malleable

While Freud and his adherents accept the fact of human creativity, explaining it as a means of releasing deeper tensions, B. F. Skinner, the best known of the modern behaviorists, denies both human creativity and human purpose. Skinner is not merely a methodological behaviorist; that is, he does not say that for methodological reasons he will confine his attention to observable behavior and make no judgments beyond it. He proceeds to deny that there is any form of human spontaneity, creativity, or purpose. He believes that all forms of human behavior are analyzable in terms of causal laws, and that these can be stated fully by means of terms such as *stimulus, response, reinforcements,* and the like. He also believes that (at least above the level of a few instinctual drives) the human organism is indefinitely malleable, so that by appropriate manipulation of the environment we could bring about an ordered society in which all human affairs go smoothly and all tensions are removed. Skinner first outlined the major tenets of this theory in 1938 in *The Behavior of Organisms,* based on his extensive observations of animal behavior, notably the behavior of rats. Among his other works are *Walden Two* (1948), a novel in which he sketched a picture of his scientifically planned human Utopia; *Verbal Behavior* (1957), a book that elicited a violently critical rejoinder from Noam Chomsky, the well-known professor of linguistics; *Beyond Freedom and Dignity* (1971), an attack on the emphasis placed by much recent humanistic literature on the need for human freedom and autonomy; and more recently an article in *Saturday Review,* "On 'Having' a Poem," in which he contends that writing a poem is no more "creative" than a woman's having a child or a hen's laying an egg. In short, Skinner rejects not only the rationalistic and voluntaristic models of man, but also the Freudian model. The human psyche has no (or virtually no) fixed structure. It responds automatically to external stimuli according to determinate (or theoretically determinable) laws. And it can be molded in almost any way that one might wish by altering the environment.

What emerges is a plea for, and a theory to support, total psychosocial engineering by scientific means. It should be stressed that Skinner is strongly and consistently opposed to punitive measures of any sort in the control of behavior. He believes that if men were properly conditioned and reinforced, there would be no occasion for punishment. One major objection to theories of freedom, in Skinner's view, is that they encourage the idea that the individual is responsible for his "bad" conduct and is therefore properly subject to punishment. Moreover, his major justification for total scientific control of behavior is that, since human behavior is totally controlled by the environment in any event, the choice is not between control and absence of control; it is between scientific control and random control.

Objections to Skinner's Model

If the voluntarist position goes to extremes in one direction, as I have argued, Skinner seems to me to go to extremes in the other. Without attempting a systematic critique, I would like to put forward several grounds of objection.

First, there is an important piece of historical evidence that seems to have been largely ignored. I refer to the fact that for a long time man's conception of the world was anthropomorphic. Mythical thought was largely animistic. Gods and spirits, conceived as creative and purposive, were believed to control the course of nature. Even Aristotle's relatively sophisticated view of the physical world construed it teleologically. Let us concede without further ado that thanks to the work of scientists, philosophers, and others, we now know an anthropomorphic view of physical nature to be mistaken. But the question remains how the mistake could have occurred in the first place. It seems obvious that because man regarded himself as a purposive and creative being, he projected his own image upon the world. If man's self-image was in fact mistaken—if he is not creative or purposive—where could he have acquired the concepts of creativity and purpose that he projected onto nature? I think the answer is clear: he could never have gotten them at all. In short, the fact that anthropomorphic views of nature were widely held, and that they comprised concepts of creativity and purpose, shows that man himself is a creative and purposive animal. He must be. If he made up these concepts out of whole cloth, this would only prove the same point more dramatically.

Second, there is a logical problem with respect to Skinner's use of his own terms. Chomsky put the matter succinctly in his review of Skinner's *Verbal Behavior* (a review that became better known, I think, than the book itself). Granting that terms like stimulus, response, and reinforcement are reasonably well-defined when applied to relatively simple experiments with rats, Chomsky called attention to the difficulty

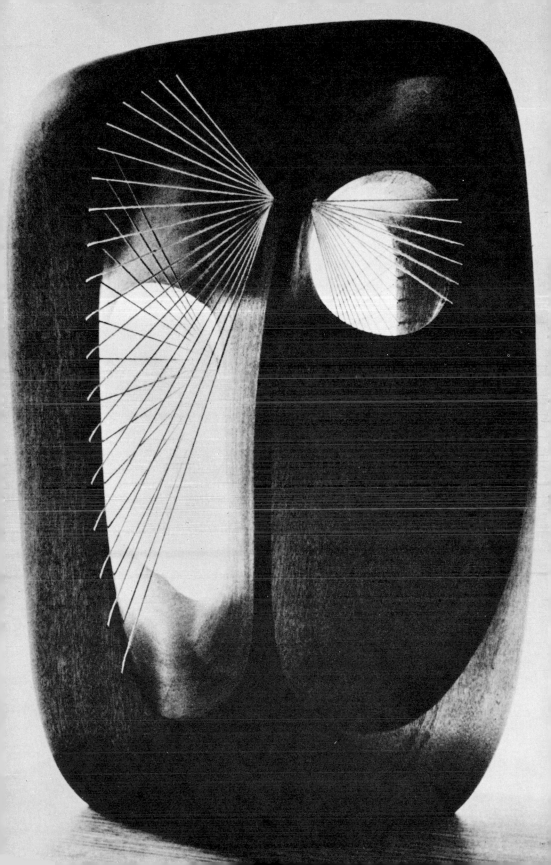

of defining them adequately when applied to more complex types of behavior:

> We must decide, first of all, whether any physical event to which the organism is capable of reacting is to be called a stimulus on a given occasion, or only one to which the organism in fact reacts; and correspondingly, we must decide whether any part of behavior is to be called a response, or only one connected with stimuli in lawful ways. Questions of this sort pose something of a dilemma for the experimental psychologist. If he accepts the broad definitions, characterizing any physical event impinging on the organism as a stimulus and any part of the organism's behavior as a reponse, he must conclude that behavior has not been demonstrated to be lawful. [If he accepts] the narrower definitions, then the behavior is lawful by definition . . . but this fact is of limited significance, since most of what the animal does will simply not be considered behavior.

This is a serious objection. If it seems overly technical, let me refer the reader to my earlier remarks about definitions. If definitions are allowed to shift at will, anyone can prove anything he likes. Skinner has never replied to this criticism or modified his own language to meet the difficulty, pleading that to reply to Chomsky he himself would have to bone up on the topics of generative grammar and structuralism, these being among Chomsky's interests. But neither of these topics bears on Chomsky's logical question about Skinner's use of words.

Consider the following passage from Skinner's *Beyond Freedom and Dignity*, where he asserts that "in operant conditioning the purpose of a skilled movement of the hand is to be found in the consequences which follow it. A pianist neither acquires nor executes the behavior of playing a scale smoothly because of a prior intention of doing so. Smoothly played scales are reinforcing for many reasons and they select skilled movements." This statement is either false or circular, as anyone who has tried to learn to play scales smoothly and failed surely knows. Indeed, without the concepts of intention and purpose—which Skinner wishes to eliminate—it is impossible to make any distinction between success and failure. If you take the actual outcome of any activity as equivalent to the purpose or intention of the actor, then no purpose can ever fail; by definition, the purpose *is* the outcome. And if there can be no such thing as failure, there can be no such thing as success.

This leads to a third objection. Skinner makes value judgments, notably the judgment that his scheme is preferable to alternatives. Yet he has removed any basis for making value judgments of any sort, including this one. We cannot found any norm on the concept of human nature because, for Skinner, human nature is entirely malleable. What has no nature has no norm. We cannot found any norm on anyone's purpose or intent—either Skinner's or anyone else's—because there are no purposes and no intentions. There are only *consequences*. What happens happens. The only escape from this impasse is to attribute validity covertly to some purposes but not to others. And this is what Skinner does. Society can be designed by Skinner's planners; their plans could be carried out successfully; the results would be superior to any alternative. This is the main thrust of the whole argument. Yet there is no basis in Skinner's premises for ascribing any validity to such an argument. His own theory serves, if it is consistently applied, to cut the ground out from under his own feet.

I am reminded of two general observations, one modern and the other ancient: Whitehead's remark that "scientists animated by the purpose of proving that they are purposeless constitute an interesting subject for study," and Epicurus' statement, many centuries ago, that "he who says that all things happen by necessity can hardly find fault with the one who denies that all happens by necessity; for on his own theory this very argument is voiced by necessity."

Finally, we come back to the point mentioned in the first chapter. Marcel asserts that men are affected by the idea or image they have of themselves. And psychiatrist Leon Eisenberg supports this view, claiming that theories about the nature of man can have the effect of self-fulfilling prophecies. Skinner denies this. In *Beyond Freedom and Dignity*, he asserts:

> No theory changes what it is a theory about. Nothing is changed because we look at it, talk about it, or analyze it in a new way. Keats drank confusion to Newton for analyzing the rainbow, but the rainbow remained as beautiful as ever and became for many even more beautiful. Man has not changed because we look at him, talk about him, and analyze him scientifically.

Plainly, there is a flat disagreement here. But we should note that whereas Eisenberg cites specific cases, Skinner argues by extrapolation from a model. Skinner takes as his normative model the procedures of physical science as applied to non-human objects. He argues by analogy. Because human knowledge of non-human objects does not affect the behavior of such objects, he concludes that the same must also hold true of man himself. But he has not looked at actual cases of human behavior to see if this is true, or even to see whether there might be ground for doubt. Here is a clear example of the way in which preconceived models affect and deflect thinking, including scientific thinking. Perhaps Skinner would say that as a scientist he has been conditioned to view everything in terms of its susceptibility to analysis by scientific method. Although this may explain his mode of thinking, it does not validate it. That is, it would allow us to answer the question, "Why does Skinner hold the views he does?" But it would not throw light on the more important question, "Should we accept Skinner's views as sound?"

Are Skinner's Views Sound?

Skinner's views may be considered in several aspects by way of illustration. First, they constitute a piece of behavior; that is, behavior by Professor Skinner. Are Skinner's own theories of behavior adequate to describe, explain, and predict his own behavior? There has been debate on this, but let us accept Skinner's own assertion that he "has" his lectures and does not "create" them. If Skinner's views are accepted as sufficient for the causal analysis (i.e., the description, explanation, and prediction) of all behavior, including Skinner's own, a second problem arises: we have no criteria for making distinctions within the total field of human behavior. So far, all behavior stands on a par. It is all describable, explainable, and predictable by certain specified methods of universal application. But these methods, precisely because of their universal applicability, fail to give us any basis for distinguishing between those types of behavior that are worthy of approval, encouragement, and reinforcement and those that are not. Skinner seems sometimes to be saying that we ought to drop all such evaluative questions about behavior. But if we do that, then we cannot evaluate Skinner's own proposals. We cannot say whether Skinner's proposals are sound or unsound, reasonable or unreasonable, wise or unwise. All we can do is observe them, explain them, and predict that Skinner will (almost certainly) continue to make them.

What Skinner has done, broadly speaking, is to put forward a *causal theory* of behavior in general and then to give it (tacitly) an *evaluative aspect*, for which the theory itself (if taken seriously) provides no basis. He has, in effect, mistaken a causal analysis for an evaluative assessment—or, more accurately, has tried to ground evaluative recommendations on a causal hypothesis. This cannot be done. Or rather, it cannot be done legitimately. It is impossible to eliminate evaluation and assessment from human intercourse. They, too, are parts of human behavior. And evaluative behavior calls not only for causal explanation but for the critical evaluation of our evaluations.

Suppose it were shown to be possible to convert human society into a society as orderly, as efficient, and as generally harmonious as a colony of ants. Would that be desirable? This is the key question. But a purely causal theory of behavior, like Skinner's, provides no criteria by which we could give an answer. The fundamental objection to Skinner's view is not that he is wrong in his estimate of human nature—though I believe he is—but that he gives us no basis for raising or deciding any questions of right and wrong, correctness and incorrectness, or even truth and falsity. In this aspect Skinner's position resembles the position he most vehemently attacks. Skinner, like Sartre, holds that man has no determinate nature but can become what he chooses. They differ as to the *agency* and *mechanics* of choice. For Sartre, the individual makes his own character by his own choices. For Skinner, the experts do the choosing; they manipulate the environment and the individual responds. One view calls itself "humanistic," the other "scientific." But if we look behind the adjectives, we are bound to ask a practical question: Where are the *criteria* by which the operative choices are to be guided and evaluated? It turns out, I think, that there are none, in either case.

Marx: Man as Productive

Another view of man quite different from Freud's or Skinner's emerged in the nineteenth century, when some thinkers came to conceive of man as *homo faber*, a creature whose distinctive capacity is for making and using tools. This view, while showing appreciation for man's inventiveness, directed attention solely to his material and mechanical inventions. Marx himself seems to have conceived of man as primarily a productive animal. For him, the prevailing system of commodity production was the key to the character of all social and political institutions and cultural values.

In *The German Ideology*, Marx and Engels asserted: "We can distinguish men from animals by consciousness, religion, or whatever we like. They themselves begin to distinguish themselves from animals as soon as they begin to *produce* the means of life. . . . In producing their means of life, men indirectly produce their material life itself." In the ideal state, as envisioned by Marx, the individual would be freed from the restrictions imposed by the division of labor, so that it would become "possible for me to do this today and that tomorrow, to hunt in the morning, to fish in the afternoon, to carry on cattle-breeding in the evening, also to criticize the food—just as I please—without becoming either hunter, fisherman, shepherd or critic." But this ideal state of affairs was seen to be dependent on restructuring the productive apparatus. For Marx, the first concern is the material conditions of life, on which everything else depends. In his "materialism" he stood side by side with the dominant outlook of nineteenth-century capitalism itself.

The distinguishing aspect of man here is his ability to produce the means of life. Marx rightly called attention to the great importance of economic factors in historical development. In doing so, however, he adopted (at least in the writings published in his lifetime) something very close to the model of *economic* man inherited from Adam Smith. As Peter Drucker says:

> Every organized society is built upon a concept of the nature of man, and of his function and place in society. Whatever its truth as a picture of human nature, this concept always gives a true picture of the society which recognizes and identifies itself with it. . . . The concept of man as an "economic animal" is the true symbol of the societies of bourgeois capitalism and of Marxist socialism, which see in the free exercise of man's economic activity the means toward the realization of their aims.

In this view, primacy is given to man's concern for survival and material well-being. The model has had great influence, not only in the fields of economic and political theory, but in other fields as well. It has, for example, colored the approach of many anthropologists to the study of primitive cultures. The model of economic man fits closely with a model that can be derived from biological evolution. If biological evolution is regarded as a struggle for survival in which capacity for adaptation to the environment plays a fundamental part, it is easy to view human cultural evolution in the same light. Many anthropologists today treat human culture as a form of adaptation by means of which human societies come to terms with their environment and learn to make use of natural resources for their welfare.

The model is in many respects useful and enlightening, but it has its limitations. The criterion of success in biological evolution is the survival of the species. If the concept of adaptation is taken over into the field of human culture, the effect is to interpret all forms of human activity in terms of one criterion: survival value. Material welfare can be brought under the model by construing survival broadly as including more than bare subsistence. A society that has acquired techniques for accumulating and preserving food, for more effective hunting, for agriculture and the domestication of animals, for shelter against storm, or for easing the burden of labor, has thereby acquired a reserve strength that enables it better to survive the vicissitudes of nature. And the same view can be applied to weapons of war, for although these may not contribute to the survival of the enemy, they contribute to the survival of the tribe itself. Difficulties arise, however, when one tries to extend this model to religion, myth, art, ornaments, games, and social rituals. To interpret such activities in terms of survival value or material usefulness is difficult, if not impossible. They come to be seen, therefore, as peripheral activities, or even aberrations, irrelevant to the main business of life. Yet, if the concept of adaptation is broadened to make room for such activities, it loses its original significance and becomes almost empty.

Material Abundance as the Ultimate Good

Another consequence of the model of economic man is that it encourages the idea that material abundance is the ultimate good. Hence we are led easily to suppose that expansion and growth may be pursued without limit, and that the highest function of man is to produce and consume as many goods and services as possible. Historian David Potter has persuasively argued that the institution of high-pressure advertising has influenced the American character toward the goal of steadily expanding consumption of material goods.

The suggestion that Marx accepted the model of economic man (as put forward by Drucker) will surely be challenged at least as an oversimplification, if not as a serious error. But I do not think it is a point we need get into here. Theories about Marx's views on the nature of man, as well as his views on history and the role of revolution, have undergone considerable revision in recent years, and it would be impossible to cover the complexities of the debates here. In any case, my concern is primarily with the model itself and its impact upon our own society. Many writers have attacked the model, and I myself have never found it adequate. But nobody can question the fact that it has been influential and that it still is influential, even in fields (like the study of tribal societies) far removed from current political controversies.

CHAPTER SEVEN

MAN AS INVENTOR

THE RATIONALIST OR INTELLECTUALIST model of the great classical philosophers has little or no influence today, but the other models I have discussed are very much alive. I believe that therein lies a primary reason for the confusions of our time—the fact that, instead of a dominant model of man, we have a set of different models that clash with one another. Each of the models calls attention to an important aspect of human activity or experience, but in my judgment, each construes the whole on the basis of a part. I wish now to consider another model that seems to be emerging. It lays stress on man's *inventiveness*. It sees man's power of invention and imagination as a common factor in all his activities—his knowings, his actings, and his makings in all situations. More comprehensive and flexible than any of the models considered thus far, it offers the hope of a solution to some of our dilemmas.

Since the days of the Greeks human inventiveness has been associated with the arts and crafts. The recognition that inventiveness plays a vital role in all knowledge came relatively late. The American pragmatists moved in this direction, notably C. S. Peirce and John Dewey. Peirce stressed the importance of imagination in the extention of scientific knowledge:

When a man desires ardently to know the truth, his first effort will be to imagine what that truth can be. He cannot prosecute his pursuit long without finding that imagination unbridled is sure to carry him off the track. Yet nevertheless it remains true that there is, after all, nothing but imagination that can ever supply him an inkling of the truth. He can stare stupidly at phenomena; but in the absence of imagination they will not connect themselves together in any rational way. . . .

It is not too much to say that next after the passion to learn there is no quality so indispensable to the successful prosecution of science as imagination. Find me a people whose early medicine is not mixed up with magic and incantations, and I will find you a people devoid of all scientific ability.

Imagination is here conceived as the power to envision possibilities not previously observed—perhaps not even directly observable. This is very different from early conceptions of imagination, which viewed it as a capacity for the reproduction or rearrangement of sense images.

John Dewey strongly attacked the traditional belief that the mind is merely passive and receptive in the process of knowing. He regarded knowledge as a transaction between mind and object. He stressed activity and practicality. His controlling model was that of technology (as distinguished from basic science), and it has been aptly said that "he summed up and was spokesman for America's expanding technological faith." Dewey explicitly attacked the visual model of knowledge. Although in my opinion he misconceived the effect of the model in some significant respects, his attack was not misdirected. The visual model does conceal the element of intellectual inventiveness involved in the anticipation of new possibilities, the framing of novel hypotheses, the construction of models, and the revision of conceptual schemes.

From early times the importance of technical ingenuity has been noted—as we have seen in Aeschylus' *Prometheus Bound*. But technical ingenuity was traditionally dissociated from theoretical inquiry. The fact is that the two activities, science (in the sense of systematic theoretical inquiry) and technology (or ingenious tinkering with practical problems), developed along separate paths which did not converge until well into the nineteenth century. Thus Edison for a long time was dismissed by established scientists as a mere "mechanic." It is the recent alliance between these two types of activity which accounts primarily for the sudden increase in the speed of technological change.

If this convergence has vastly complicated our immediate social, economic, political, and ecological problems, it has also been attended by some major conceptual shifts, which offer some hope of yielding a new and more adequate conception of the nature f man himself. I regard this as a matter of primary importance, because without a conception of man capable of eliciting some degree of consensus, we remain without any agreed point of reference for establishing a coherent set of values and goals.

Knowledge and Norms

One shift already making itself felt affects our fundamental concepts and models of knowledge, including scientific knowledge. This shift involves the increasing appreciation that knowledge does not begin with observed data but with the *set of norms or standards* we use for organizing data. These include norms for sorting, classifying, measuring, assessing, and ranking observed data, and also norms for making linguistic reports about our observations. To explain briefly: you could not report that a rose is red unless you had standards for identifying roses (as opposed to violets or dogs or stones), for identifying redness (as opposed to blueness or largeness or wideness), and for employing the words "rose," "red," and "is" in English.

Because this complex network of conceptual and linguistic norms is so familiar to us that we apply it automatically, we seldom notice its existence. It serves us somewhat like a pair of spectacles whose presence is ignored so long as we can see the world through them without difficulty. Even when we have occasion to realize that a conceptual network exists, we may not appreciate its normative character. It is easy to suppose that in reporting the redness of a rose, we are not making a judgment but merely recording an experience. This supposition rests, I believe, on our continued domination by a model of mind which suggests that (in an act of perceptual awareness) the mind is (or ought to be) receptive and passive. I believe that this familiar model is mistaken, and that Sir Geoffrey Vickers is essentially accurate when he says:

> The simplest discrimination—"This is a that"—(whether "that" be a cow, a contract, or a sin) is no mere finding of fact but a judgment which carves something out of the field of attention and assimilates it to a category which has been generated by previous acts of the same kind. The simplest valuation—"This should be thus"—is equally a judgment arrived at by comparing some object or event or course of events (real or imagined) with some standard which has become accepted as the appropriate norm. The simplest decision on action—

"In these circumstances this should be done"—is the selection of a response from a repertory by rules which determine what is suitable to what occasion. The categories by which we discriminate, the standards by which we value, the repertory of responses from which we select, and our rules for selection are all mental artifacts, evolved, learned, and taught by the cultural process and more or less peculiar to the culture which produces them. This process is a circular process, in which all these settings of the appreciative system are constantly being modified by their own exercise.

Vickers' view is at odds with much current philosophical theory, and his statement bristles with controversial assertions and implications. But its main thrust seems to me correct: all observation has a normative foundation, and all reports of observation include an element of evaluation and appraisal. If this is at the moment a minority view, it is gaining headway. The eminent German philosopher Ernst Cassirer writes in his major work, *The Philosophy of Symbolic Forms*, that "every *apprehension* of a particular empirical thing or specific empirical occurrence contains within it an act of *evaluation*." And the economist and social critic Kenneth Boulding has asserted that in what we call rational behavior, a man's "response is not to an immediate stimulus but to an image of the future filtered through an elaborate value system."

To the man of practical experience, or to the student who has not yet had his thought-patterns hardened by accepted theoretical dogmas, there should be no difficulty in such statements. They seem to be reasonably accurate accounts of what we normally experience when we engage in the process called *knowing*. We treat the object in terms of categories and models brought forward from past experience; we envisage future possibilities; we apply language according to habitual usage; and we make constant assessments and evaluations. If there are difficulties, it is, I think, because we are in the habit of accepting (usually uncritically) certain familiar doctrines about empirical knowledge, such as these: what is actually presented to us here and now is the basic datum; unobserved possibilities are problematical; cognition and valuation are separate processes; and descriptive reports and normative judgments must be carefully distinguished. These are all doctrines inherited from theories about knowledge—theories, incidentally, that appear to rest on very dubious foundations in light of recent psychological investigations. If, as I believe, every observation involves an act of evaluation and even the simplest descriptive statement presupposes a complex set of norms, then the picture is materially changed. And the change involves not only our views about knowing but our views about man himself.

Cassirer and Jonas: Man as Symbol-Maker

Cassirer has recommended that we conceive of man as neither a rational animal nor a tool-making animal, but rather as a creature who makes and uses symbols. This conception focuses on what is almost certainly man's most extraordinary and unique accomplishment, his capacity to make and use language. Hans Jonas has suggested that to avoid possible controversies over the concept of "language," we might conceive man as an image-maker, since the capacity to make representations of things implies that man is "potentially a speaking, thinking, inventing, in short 'symbolical' being."

If we build on the fact that man is a *symbolical* animal, several important consequences follow. In the first place, we are no longer impelled to conceive of man in terms of any one particular interest or need. We do not have to give primacy to his desire for knowledge, his demand for autonomy of the will, his need to reconcile the tension of conflicting impulses, or his concern for survival and material welfare. Instead, man is conceived of in terms of a capacity that is vitally implicated in all his activities, including those concerned with meeting each of his particular needs. We are, therefore, in a position to do justice to all types of human concern, in their multiplicity and variety, without having to assume that one of them must be dominant under all circumstances. Second, we can establish a connection (instead of a disjunction) among man's science, technology, art, literature, religion, philosophy, social activities, politics, rituals, games and so forth. All typically human activities are symbolical activities. The highest powers of abstract thought depend on man's ability to construct and manipulate symbols, as does the child's capacity for make-believe.

The most familiar example of a complex symbol-system is language itself. Young children can learn a language without difficulty—a remarkable intellectual feat. It has plausibly been suggested that the difficulty adults find in learning new languages lies not in the difficulty of the new symbolism but in breaking away from the acquired habits of the old. Even the most backward peoples have speech, often of very sophisticated construction. By contrast, the symbolical capacities of animals appear to be small or nonexistent. Animals can of course use sounds and gestures to express feelings, and they can make and respond to signals. They can also be taught to respond to signal systems devised by man—to press a bar to obtain food, for example, at the flash of a light or the sound of a bell. Perhaps some animal can even be taught to use man-made symbol systems, at least in a simplified form. Recent experiments with chimpanzees at least suggest the possibility. But no animal except man has shown any capacity for creating an artificial symbol system.

To say that symbolic systems like human language are artificial is to say that they are human artifacts. It thus becomes clear that the distinction between the *natural* and the *artificial* or *conventional* cannot be invoked (as it was by the classical philosophers and by Rousseau) as a general criterion of intrinsic rightness, propriety, or worth. Man has a natural capacity, due apparently to the extraordinary physiological development of his brain, to create artificial things. His artifacts include not merely physical objects like tools, machines, buildings, and statues, but also symbolic systems and normative systems of various kinds.

Every symbolic system is a system of norms governing the behavior of those who use it. If you depart significantly from the accepted standards (norms) of social behavior, you incur the risk of disapproval and the possible imposition of a penalty. If you depart too far from the accepted standards (norms) of linguistic behavior, the mildest and probably the most common "penalty" is that you are considered to be talking nonsense and what you say is ridiculed or ignored. There can, of course, be more stringent consequences for linguistic misbehavior. Blasphemy was at one time considered a serious offense, and obscene language may still be penalized, though a workable definition is difficult to formulate—all the more so because the social standards (norms) of acceptability in this regard have changed so dramatically in recent years. But slanderous or libelous utterances are actionable, as are fraudulent representations and other types of speech deemed socially dangerous. It is true that in such cases the norms involved are not linguistic norms. But the point is that verbal behavior, like all kinds of behavior, is subject to various norms of which the norm of "correct" usage is one particular type. The creation of normative systems is an aspect of the symbolic process, resting upon man's remarkable capacity for invention.

That the pursuit of scientific knowledge is norm-dependent has been obscured, almost fatally, I think, by the ambiguity of the word *empirical*. Science is empirical in that it is governed by the general maxim that we should always check our theories against the observable data —that we should never make the "facts" conform to preconceived theories but should make our theories conform to the "facts." Now it is clear that this maxim is a normative principle. It tells us what we *ought* to do. The justification for the empirical maxim lies in the common human experience that if you disregard actualities, you invite confusion or disaster, or both.

"Empiricism" vs. "The Empirical Attitude"

Empiricism is something else. The term *empiricism* has come to refer to a particular type of theory concerning the origins of our ideas, specifically the theory that all ideas are derived, directly or indirectly, from the data of sense experience. Several points need to be made. First, empiricism is a theory about the relationship between knowledge and experience. Such a theory may or may not be empirically based. One might subscribe to the empiricist doctrine not on the basis of observed data but on purely theoretical grounds. Thus *empiricism need not be empirical*. Second, there is a serious question whether empiricism is true. This topic is currently under active debate, since many psychologists and an increasing number of philosophers and scientists think it is untrue, or only marginally true. Third, there is the question whether, assuming that empiricism gives a true account of the psychological origins (i.e., causes) of our ideas, it provides any criterion for distinguishing those ideas and beliefs that are valid (i.e., trustworthy, reliable, rationally acceptable) from those that are not. For several reasons already given, I believe it does not. In any case, to be an empiricist is one thing; to be empirical is quite another.

One illustration may be useful. The author of the Book of Job was not an *empiricist*. He did not develop any systematic theory about the origins of human knowledge; if he had done so, he would undoubtedly have attributed knowledge primarily to divine revelation. But he was thoroughly *empirical* in attitude. The prevailing theory in his day, as reflected in the views put forward by his friends, was that those who obey God's laws are materially rewarded and those who disobey are punished. This theory entailed the view that anybody who suffers must necessarily have sinned. Job saw that this theory did not fit the facts of human experience, since the virtuous man sometimes suffers and the vicious man sometimes prospers. Hence Job challenged the theory. As a result of his challenge, the theory was destroyed. By the time of Ecclesiastes, it was accepted that the race is not always to the swift nor the battle to the strong, nor prosperity always to the man of virtue.

The empirical attitude is thus important for poets, dramatists, and religious writers as well as for scientists. It is also to be noted that although men of science for many centuries past have been empirical, few of them have been empiricists in the philosophical sense. As White-

head remarked, science continued undisturbed by the fact that Hume had refuted it. Yet many writers still confuse *philosophical empiricism* with the *empirical attitude*, either condemning science and technology because they associate them with dogmatic empiricism or adopting a rigid empiricism because they consider it "scientific" and therefore intellectually respectable. Both positions are equally unjustified.

Consequences of Man-as-Inventor Model

Let us consider briefly some specific consequences of the view that man is an inventive being. If we treat social norms as products of man's natural inventiveness and as practical necessities for social cooperation and communication, we can no longer condemn them on principle as being "artificial." Some norms may be oppressive and unjust; others may not. Each case has to be considered on its merits. Nor can we accept the view that conformity to social norms is bad (or good) in and of itself. We have to recognize that routine is a necessary part of life. It does not merely serve as a force for stability; it also makes it possible for each of us to do many things in habitual ways, thereby freeing us to devote special attention to those matters that, at any given moment, are of special importance. Nobody can attend to everything at once. To be sure, social routine can be static and oppressive, just as personal habits can be stultifying, even destructive. But every case has to be looked at with concern for the particular factors involved and the alternate possibilities.

The quest for knowledge also requires inventiveness, especially in the envisioning of possibilities, the framing of hypotheses, the devising of experiments for testing hypotheses, and the like. This does not in any sense imply that facts can be disregarded or that objectivity is destroyed. It means that we recognize the important fact that all observation is (in N. R. Hanson's phrase) "theory-laden." The concept of a "fact" as a pure datum which stands by itself and presents itself to an emptily receptive mind is now seen to be a theoretical invention. It was produced by man and was widely accepted for a long time, but it is now proved by experience to be false.

Finally, as to moral ideals, these too are *inventions*—but none the worse for it. What we are coming to see is that fictions and ideal models of various types play a vital role in all our thinking, including scientific thinking. It is becoming clear that our habitual distrust of fictions and ideal models is itself based on the acceptance of an ideal model, namely the old conception of knowledge as ideally consisting of the pure confrontation of an object by an empty and unclouded mind. This ideal model of knowledge, long dominant in our thinking, now proves to create many more difficulties and anomalies than those it was designed to solve. Having tested it, we must now reject it. Moral ideals are to be tested in the same way, by considering their implications and observing them (as far as we can) in operation. The difficulty is, of course, that moral ideals are projections. They are envisioned possibilities rather than actualities, and we cannot know for certain whether a given moral ideal is sound unless and until we have tried it out. But there is no more reason to insist on absolute certainty in the moral realm than in science itself, where we have learned to act on probabilities while recognizing them as such.

CHAPTER EIGHT

MAN'S SEARCH FOR MEANING

IF WE CONCEIVE OF MAN as an inventive animal and consider that all his knowledge, including his scientific knowledge, constitutes a kind of inventing, we can see the importance of metaphysical inquiry. The dominant metaphor or model makes all the difference. As long as we think of knowing as an activity in which the mind is essentially passive and receptive—as long as we suppose that the ideal model of truly "objective" knowledge consists of an empty mind, freed of all preconceptions, blankly confronting data presented for its awareness—we naturally distrust metaphysical speculations. Given this model, we readily conceive of metaphysical inquiry as an effort to discern, by some mysterious process of intellectual intuition, preexistent truths which transcend concrete experience and observation. In brief, if the mind is conceived as a mental eye, metaphysical investigations may appear as attempts to "see" what is invisible. If we shift the model, the situation changes. We may then recognize that the mind is neither blank nor merely passive, that there is no such thing as *presuppositionless* observation, that all awareness takes place within a conceptual framework, that both perception and thought are always colored to some degree by emotional attitudes, and that any ideal model of knowing (including the traditional model) is an imaginative construction. On this basis, the role of metaphysical inquiry is to uncover the patterns and assumptions underlying our own outlook on the world, testing them for adequacy and coherence and, if necessary, devising new categories, models and conceptual schemes to serve us better. Whitehead's conception of speculative philosophy follows this pattern:

> Speculative philosophy can be defined as the endeavour to frame a coherent, logical, necessary system of general ideas in terms of which every element of our experience can be interpreted. Here "interpretation" means that each element shall have the character of a particular instance of the general scheme.
>
> Thus speculative philosophy embodies the method of the working hypothesis. The purpose of the working hypothesis for philosophy is to coordinate the current expressions of human experience, in common speech, in social institutions, in actions, in the principles of the various special sciences, elucidating harmony and exposing discrepancies. . . . Such an hypothesis directs observation, and decides upon the mutual relevance of various types of evidence. In short, it prescribes method.

In this view, metaphysical inquiry is not directed, in the first instance, at the world but at our own conceptual apparatus. It becomes a kind of self-critical assessment of our own habitual ways of looking at the world and of classifying and organizing experience. It is tested by its adequacy in performing the required function. If an habitual conceptual scheme or orientation serves to conceal or suppress some kind of experience, if it is incoherent or inconsistent, if it generates an intolerable number of anomalies, it must be discarded in favor of some alternative. Thus the function of metaphysics is seen as critical and inventive.

Why Is Metaphysical Inquiry Important?

Why is this kind of inquiry important? For the simple reason that all items in experience are interconnected and all thought involves presuppositions. Thought and language are necessarily abstract because they necessarily select certain items for attention, leaving out other things. We therefore need to guard ourselves constantly against mistaking abstractions of thought and language for a full account of concrete reality. The tacit assumptions involved in habitual thinking are also apt to be forgotten. It follows, according to Whitehead, that "in the absence of some understanding of the final nature of things . . . all science suffers from the vice that it may be combining various propositions which tacitly presuppose inconsistent backgrounds. No science can be more secure than the unconscious metaphysics which it tacitly presupposes. All reasoning, apart from some metaphysical reference, is vicious."

In brief, all forms of knowledge tacitly presuppose metaphysics. That is to say, they make certain assumptions about the ultimate nature of things—including the nature of man. There is no way to avoid assumptions of this sort. It is possible to ignore them or even to pretend that they are not being made, which is like perpetually adding to a tower without checking its foundations. But it is also possible to avoid this mistake, and this is precisely the mission of speculative philosophy, or metaphysics. The same considerations would apply, of course, in areas other than the sciences. Whitehead would have agreed, I think, that it is impossible to put forward any political or moral theories without making some assumptions about the nature of man. The concept or model may be awkward; it may be slippery; it may be indefinite. But since we cannot avoid employing some model of man, tacitly if not explicitly, it is important to be aware of what we are doing and to consider what implications may be latent in the models we have available for use.

The model of man as an inventive and symbolical animal therefore invites a kind of critical assessment of our knowledge which the earlier models either prohibited or discounted. A contributing factor here was undoubtedly the pervasive faith in progress, especially faith in the continuous advancement of human welfare through the advance of science and technology. Given such a faith, which I have likened to the *hybris* feared by the Greek tragedians, there was little inclination toward caution. Some, like Whitehead himself, saw the need for reconsidering a number of accepted philosophical doctrines and for revising established theories about the nature and procedures of scientific knowledge. This reassessment has gathered headway, and we may expect it to go much further, though its full implication cannot yet be fully foreseen.

We come now to a related matter, the problem mentioned earlier, of the "wholeness" of human personality. Gordon Allport was particularly concerned with this question throughout his long career as a psychologist. In a lecture given in 1938 he noted that whereas scientific psychologists have found the subject baffling and obscure, great literary artists seem to have little difficulty portraying characters who are psychologically both complex and unified. Allport questioned whether the study of human personality properly belonged to the sciences or to the arts. He concluded that it belonged to both and recommended that psychologists learn from literature and artists from psychology. His principal injunction, however, which he repeated elsewhere, was that the problem of wholeness (that is, integration of personality) must be studied by examining individuals (either actual or fictional) and not by manipulating general concepts or linguistic abstractions. He made important contributions of his own to the theory of personality, and other psychologists and psychiatrists of "humanistic" bent have done the same, including such men as Abraham Maslow, Rollo May, Erik Erikson, Viktor Frankl, and Robert Jay Lifton. Despite some variations in viewpoint, all these writers appear to agree that every individual has a psychological need for what Bernard Shaw described as "a clear conception of life in the light of an intelligible theory." This is a point on which the great masters of literature have been virtually unanimous. Man needs order in his world, and he needs to find meaning in his own existence. When a man cannot comprehend his world or his place in it, the results are apt to be traumatic.

One of the most famous examples is, of course, the Book of Job. It is sometimes thought that Job's misery was caused by his physical sufferings and his material losses, but an attentive reading of the text shows far more. What causes Job's despair is the shattering of his intellectual and spiritual world. Job is portrayed as a man who has shared the established belief that man's function is to obey God's law, and that for this he will be rewarded with prosperity. But in Job's case, the rule does not hold true: Job is innocent, yet he suffers. The unknown author of the book clearly wished to challenge the accepted doctrine and did so by writing a dramatic poem of great depth and beauty. We know from experience that the good man does not always prosper, nor the bad man always suffer. Hence the prevailing theory, however comfortable to our own moral and religious sense, does not appear to fit the facts. The author of the book made his point by dramatizing the experience of the man who suffers without having done wrong. In this situation he is desperately perplexed and bewildered. Job's friends argue that since he is suffering, he must have sinned. But Job cannot concede this. And he demands two things. The first is that he be allowed to confront God directly—an extraordinary demand that is granted. God speaks to Job out of the whirlwind. The second demand is for an explanation. If Job has sinned, he feels entitled to know what he has done wrong; if he has not sinned, he feels entitled to know why he has been punished. But this demand for an explanation is denied. God, speaking to Job, insists that His ways are beyond human comprehension. And Job, having experienced God's presence, submits.

Observe that God might easily have told Job that it had all been done

to test his faith, the message conveyed in the prologue to the book itself. But God makes no mention of this when he speaks to Job from the whirlwind. Moreover, God repudiates the view put forward by Job's friends. Hence it seems evident that the final few lines of the book, stating that Job was ultimately rewarded, are (as most scholars agree) a later emendation and not part of the original. The whole thrust of the book, at least in the poetic central section, is to the effect that the good are not always rewarded, nor are the vicious always made to suffer. Why this is so, man cannot say; but he must accept the fact, as did Job. Thereafter, the view of Job's friends was abandoned, as we can see in Ecclesiastes. The author of the Book of Job knew clearly that no man could undergo so severe a shock to his habitual beliefs as Job experienced without a shattering emotional impact. And the drama portrays exactly that. Job is restored to tranquility, but only by God's majesty as immediately disclosed to him.

Man's deep need to comprehend his world is also reflected in much primitive mythology. A dramatic myth provides a kind of model by which man can come to terms with the vicissitudes of human life. And myths give rise to concepts. Paul Ricoeur's book, *The Symbolism of Evil*, discusses the slow development, against the background of myth, of the concepts of defilement, sin, and guilt—leading ultimately to the modern concept of individual responsibility. If we put aside the model of economic man and also the rigid empiricist model of human knowledge, we can begin to understand the significance of myth, ritual, and religion. All are concerned with man's persistent search for understanding.

Something to Believe In

Jumping to more modern times, we may start by noting the assertion of Dostoevsky's Grand Inquisitor that "the secret of man's being is not only to live but to have something to live for." George Orwell, himself a socialist of sorts, explained the attraction of communism to British intellectuals in the 1930s on this ground: "But what do you achieve, after all, by getting rid of such primal things as patriotism and religion? You have not necessarily got rid of the need for *something to believe in*. . . . So, after all, the 'Communism' of the English intellectual is something explicable enough. It is the patriotism of the deracinated."

If deracination—a feeling of uprootedness and emptiness—is a major factor in the spreading phenomenon called alienation in our day, we may attribute it, at least in large measure, to the fact that our society has failed to give the younger generation either a coherent metaphysical framework or a compelling set of values. In *The Rebel*, Camus discusses "metaphysical rebellion," remarking—rightly, I believe—that the rebel "is seeking, without knowing it, a moral philosophy or a religion."

There is considerable talk today about *nihilism*, sometimes with the implication that nihilism is the negation of all values. This seems to me a clear mistake. What is called nihilism is not an absence of values, but the lack of any criteria for ranking them or choosing among them. I disagree strongly with those writers who speak of the experience of nothingness as if nothingness were something that could be encountered and as if nihilism grew out of such experiences. What is metaphorically called the "encounter with nothingness" is, I think, the experience of being unable to make significant discriminations. Life is not empty; if anything, it is too full. But the various items of experience and the values attaching to them seem to stand all on a par with one another. In such a world, it is true that nothing makes a difference. This is not because we are confronted by nothing, but because there are no differences. In the dark all cats are black. In the darkness of nihilism all acts and all experiences are colorless because their colors are alike. Nothing stands out beyond the fleeting sensations of the moment, which are gone before they can be grasped. In brief, it is not the world that thrusts nothingness upon us. It is we who project "nothingness" and "meaninglessness" upon the world when we lose hold of any conceptual and normative framework by which to organize our experience and make discriminations.

I do not deny that such experiences occur, and that they are traumatic. What I am saying is that they are due to *symbolic dislocation*. They are further evidence of the depth of man's need for comprehensible order and meaning. It is possible, of course, that the experience of symbolic dislocation can lead to deeper insights. The mystics pass through the "dark night of the soul" and emerge into what they experience as a more profound state of understanding and wisdom. Perhaps Job was a case in point. On a more mundane level, some degree of symbolic dislocation occurs whenever an accepted model or conceptual scheme is found to create so many anomalies that it needs to be replaced. The development of radically new outlooks and orientations, in science and elsewhere, seems typically to involve a process of this kind. But major conceptual shifts are apt to be slow and difficult precisely because they involve a major reorientation of outlook. Intellectual habits once established are very hard to change, and change can be deeply disturbing.

Meaning and Identity

The search for meaning is also involved in the individual's quest for his own identity. An integral dimension of the individual's identity is the quality of his relatedness to the context in which he finds himself. Marcus Aurelius knew this: "He who does not know what the world is, does not know where he is. And he who does not know for what purpose the world exists, does not know who he is, nor what the world is." In recent years, Erik Erikson, who has concerned himself especially with problems of identity—and who coined the phrase "identity crisis" only to see it degraded into an empty slogan—has consistently stressed the intimate connection between the development of a person's identity and the development of his general outlook upon the world. Erikson, like Allport, feels the need to study concrete individuals in their diversity as opposed to talking about human "wholeness" on the basis of fashionable verbal abstractions. As for alienation, he says:

> I, for one, have never been able to accept the claim that in mercantile culture or in agricultural culture, or, indeed, in book culture, man was in principle less "alienated" than he is in technology. It is, I believe, our own retrospective romanticism which makes us think that peasants or merchants or hunters were less determined by their techniques. To put it in terms of what must be studied concertedly: in every technology and in every historical period there are types of individuals who ("properly" brought up) can combine the dominant techniques with their identity development and *become* what they *do*.

"We cannot know what technological conformity does *to* man," he further observes, "unless we know what it does *for* him."

It follows that we cannot hold (with Plato) that individual specialization is inherently natural and good, or (with Marx) that specialization is inherently artificial and oppressive. Each of these views overly generalizes, ignoring the many diversities of individual personality. Generalizations must be directed at those aspects of human nature which seem common to all men after allowing for individual diversity.

The Viennese psychiatrist Viktor Frankl concludes, on the basis of his own experience as a prisoner in a Nazi death-camp during World War II, that there are three kinds of human neuroses: psychogenic, which are conventionally labeled as such and are commonly dealt with by psychoanalytic theories; somatogenic, which arise from physiological disturbances; and noogenic, which "result from the frustration of the will-to-meaning, from what I have called existential frustration, or from the existential vacuum." In Frankl's view, "man is neither dominated by the will-to-pleasure nor by the will-to-power, but by what I should like to call man's *will-to-meaning*; that is to say, his deep-seated striving and struggling for a higher and ultimate meaning to his existence. Man is groping and longing for a meaning to be fulfilled by him and by him alone; in other words, for what we would call a mission."

This view does not entail the conclusion of Plato and Aristotle that man's highest form of self-realization is found in the contemplation of final and unchanging truth. But it confirms the view that when meaning and purpose are lost, pathological conditions ensue. As long as an individual feels a sense of individual mission that gives significance to his life, he can survive hardships, even tortures. In Nietzsche's words, "He who has a *why* to live can bear with almost any *how*."

Robert Jay Lifton, an eminent American psychiatrist who interviewed the survivors of the atom bomb at Hiroshima, seems prepared to agree with Frankl's affirmation of the psychological centrality of man's intellectual and spiritual concerns: "When I say, therefore, that we are all survivors of Hiroshima, I mean this to be more than a dramatic metaphor. I think we are all involved in a struggle to find significance and meaning in a world in which such events can occur." Lifton, on the strength of his investigations, has concluded that in the face of inevitable death, every individual is impelled to search for symbolic immortality. He seeks to identify himself with some cause or process that continues beyond his own demise, resorting to a belief in theological immortality, perhaps, or identification with his descendants, or commitment to some ongoing struggle, such as the cause of permanent revolution. Lifton regards man as a symbolical animal who views the world in terms of models and categories of his own making. Symbolic dislocation occurs when familiar categories no longer seem to apply to what is happening. In this situation, the individual can no longer cope with the world around him. Lifton asserts that "if we regard man as primarily a symbol-forming organism, we must recognize that he has constant need of meaningful inner formulation of self and world, in which his actions, and even his impulses, have some kind of 'fit' with the 'outside' as he perceives it." On this basis, he holds—and I think he is correct—that it is the apparent formlessness and incoherence of modern industrial society that creates disaffection, not its monolithic structure, as Marcuse would have it. Thus we are brought back to Marcel's claim that the present crisis of Western man is metaphysical.

Some Concluding Observations

I would like to make a few last observations to conclude what has

necessarily been the briefest of surveys of how philosophers and others have wrestled over the years with the question of man's place in things. In 1733 Alexander Pope published his poetic *Essay on Man*, including the famous couplet: "Know then thyself, presume God not to scan / The proper study of mankind is man." And in the years since, the study of man has been vigorously pursued. Vast amounts of new information have accumulated, especially in recent decades, from biology, biochemistry, biophysics, physiology, psychology, anthropology, sociology, economics, history, and various other sources. Yet an increase of information has not brought an increase in understanding. On the contrary, the more we know about man, the more mysterious he seems to become.

A number of writers have pointed out that one characteristic of our times is that man has become more problematical to himself than in any other age. We have several different conceptions and models of man, more or less carefully articulated, each reflecting a particular perspective and a particular range of interests, but the multiplicity of disciplines and the variety of approaches have tended to prevent the emergence of any single conception of human nature sufficiently comprehensive and sufficiently flexible to provide a *unifying* focus.

It is my belief that a unifying focus may be found if we stress man's capacity for inventiveness, recognizing that such inventiveness is displayed not merely in man's arts and crafts, but also in his ability to establish complex symbol systems, to make and modify social systems, and to build elaborate normative systems to guide his own behavior. The root of man's inventiveness seems to lie in his capacity—evidently correlated with his highly developed brain—to envisage *possibilities* beyond the actualities of immediate experience. Human knowledge, including scientific knowledge, reflects this capacity and depends on it. The scientific enterprise is surely one of the most sophisticated of all human contrivances. Like all other major human enterprises, it is value-oriented, goal-directed, and norm-governed. In this case the dominant values are descriptive truth and accuracy, for the achievement of which other values are—provisionally, but quite deliberately—put aside. But the ideal of scientific neutrality is itself, like all other ideals, a human invention. And like other human ideals, it is subject to abuse if its character and function are misconceived.

This view of man has many implications, far too many for me to discuss here. But let me mention a few of the more important ones.

First, stress on the inventiveness of man makes us see the need for metaphysical inquiry into the nature and coherence of our underlying preconceptions about the world, about the foundations of human knowledge, and about man himself. If there is no such thing as totally unbiased knowing—if we reject the ideal model of an empty mind passively contemplating pure data presented to pure awareness—then we must direct our primary attention to the assumptions and patterns of analysis that we bring to all our acts of knowing and judging.

Second, we come to recognize the immense importance of imagination in all human activities—imagination in the sense of the ability to construct hypotheses and ideals that go beyond what has actually been observed.

Third, the supposed gap between scientific activities and humanistic activities appears in a new light. The familiar distinction between facts and values is seen to rest on an act of abstraction that we ourselves make. Like other conceptual orderings, it is useful for some purposes, but it can be misconceived and misapplied. It is misapplied if we assume (as we have come to do by force of habit) that it reflects a fundamental distinction imposed on us by experience itself. The truth is, I think, that the varied activities of man, from his art, his myths, and his religion to his science and technology, are complementary. Every major human activity, including the search for pure and disinterested knowledge, is norm-governed and value-oriented.

Finally, this model of man allows us to do justice to man's persistent search for meaning, a need that has long since been recognized by artists and writers and that is now beginning to find support in current investigations of human personality. As a symbol-making and symbol-using animal, man finds himself disoriented if his customary symbol systems fail to fit the conditions with which he is confronted.

This analysis serves to locate the central problem rather than to solve it, since the search for meaning can produce evil as well as good. As Dostoevsky's Grand Inquisitor pointed out: the hunger for meaning and order may become so great as to drive men to sacrifice freedom in order to escape from the burden of bewildered frustration it can cause. It is easier to see the dangers than to prescribe a remedy. But I am convinced that an essential part of the remedy lies in the preservation of what Marcel calls the *philosophic spirit*.

This is a matter of attitude rather than of specific doctrine, but it is an attitude informed by active concern for the dignity of man. It requires of course that we begin by clarifying our idea of *man*—as I have attempted to do in this essay. For our ideas of knowledge, values, ethics, and religion all depend on our assumptions of man. Man depends to a great degree on the idea he has of himself, and this self-understanding cannot exist in a vacuum. Thus an understanding of man leads us necessarily to metaphysical and historical inquiry. From these we learn to live for an openness, honesty, and simplicity in our human relationships and against forces of fanaticism that threaten to debase or destroy the dignity of man. This inner attitude should manifest itself in all our actions. We still profit from the legacy of Plato and Aristotle that intellectual understanding is fundamental to man and that all wise human action depends on it.

NOTES

Introduction

General Note: That man in the modern world has become problematic to himself is widely asserted. General discussions include Arendt, *The Human Condition*; Cassirer, *Man Against Mass Society*; and Jaspers, *Man in the Modern Age*. Heschel, *Who Is Man?*, and Marcel, *Problematic Man*, reflect a religious perspective. An anthology of short selections reflecting a wide variety of views, past and present, about the nature of man is found in Fromm and Xirau, *The Nature of Man*. Several essays by scientists are included in Platt, *New Views of the Nature of Man*. An important recent book by a noted biologist is Monod's *Chance and Necessity*.

PAGE 1 Trevor-Roper's observation, from "Human Nature and Politics," *The Listener*, Dec. 10, 1953, is cited by Potter, *People and Plenty*, p. xvi, where Potter's general comment may also be found.

PAGE 2 For Plato's sketch of Protagoras, see his *Protagoras*. For Plato's interpretation of the dictum that man is the measure of all things, see his *Theaetetus*, steph. 152-62.

PAGE 2 For the familiar portrait of the Renaissance Man, see Burckhardt, *The Civilization of the Renaissance in Italy*. It is argued in Cassirer, *The Logic of the Humanities*, ch. III, that the portrait is historically valuable as a composite model even though it does not correspond with any particular individual.

PAGE 2 Aristotle, *Nicomachean Ethics*, bk. 3, ch. IV, trans. Rackham: "For the good man judges everything correctly . . . and perhaps what chiefly distinguishes the good man is that he sees the truth in each kind [of thing], being himself as it were the standard and the measure of the noble and the pleasant."

PAGE 2 On the tendency of philosophical anarchists to take an optimistic view of man, see the materials collected in Krimerman and Perry, *Patterns of Anarchy*.

PAGE 4 The rejection of bourgeois values by the *avant-garde* movement in the arts is a phenomenon occurring *within* bourgeois society and sustained by it, see Kramer, "The Age of the Avant-Garde," *Commentary*, Oct. 1972.

PAGE 4 Ferkiss, *Technological Man: The Myth and the Reality*, Mentor ed., p. 22.

PAGE 4 Lifton, *Boundaries*, pp. 37-53.

PAGE 4 Philosophy as philosophizing: Jaspers, *Way to Wisdom*, ch. I; *The Future of Mankind*, ch. I, XIII, XV.

Chapter 1

PAGE 8   Marcel, *Man Against Mass Society*, p. 20.

PAGE 8   Eisenberg, "The *Human* Nature of Human Nature," *Science*, April 14, 1972.

PAGE 9   Marcel, *Man Against Mass Society*, p. 37.

PAGE 10 Kaufman, in Schacht, *Alienation*, Anchor ed., Introductory Essay, p. xiv.

PAGE 10 Marcel, *Man Against Mass Society*, p. 39.

PAGE 11 *Youth in Turmoil*, Time-Life Books, 1969, p. 57. Among the many surveys of student activism, those of Lipset, *Revolution and Counterrevolution*, 1968, and Lipset and Schaflander, *Passion and Politics: Student Activism in America*, 1971, are especially recommended.

PAGE 12 Marcel, *Man Against Mass Society*, pp. 112-14. For the view that fanaticism may arise, not merely from blind commitment, but from agnosticism and resentful doubt, see Simon, *Philosophy of Democratic Government*, pp. 91-92.

PAGE 12 Marcel, *Man Against Mass Society*, p. 244.

PAGE 13 Marcel, *Man Against Mass Society*, p. 272 (on the need to oppose the spirit of abstraction). Cf. Whitehead, *Science and the Modern World*, ch. III, on the fallacy of misplaced concreteness.

PAGE 14 Marcel, *Man Against Mass Society*, p. 130.

PAGE 14 Thucydides, *Peloponnesian War*, bk. 3, sec. 82-83.

PAGE 14 Fuller, *The Morality of Law*, p. 19.

PAGE 15 Marcel, *Three Plays*, p. 27.

Chapter 2

General Note: Modern scientific and analytic philosophy has tended to ignore or to deny the legitimacy of analogies and metaphors in scientific thinking (see Reichenbach, *The Rise of Scientific Philosophy*). But there is increasing recognition of the fact that analogies, metaphors, and tacit models, including ideal models, play a vital role in *all* our thinking, including scientific thinking. For general discussions, see Harré, *The Principles of Scientific Thinking*; Pepper, *World Hypotheses*; and Black, *Models and Metaphors*. This fact requires a radical revision in our conceptions of human knowledge and the nature of scientific "objectivity."

PAGE 18 For the earlier phases of analytic philosophy, see Urmson, *Philosophical Analysis*. For a brief account of Wittgenstein and the later phases of the analytic movement, see Hartnack, *Wittgenstein and Modern Philosophy*.

PAGE 19 Whitehead, *Science and Modern World*, ch. II, sec viii.

PAGE 19 Descartes, *Rules for the Direction of the Mind*, Rule II and commentary (last paragraph).

PAGE 20 Aristotle, *Nichomachean Ethics*, bk. 1, ch. III. The standard empiricist doctrine that knowledge deals only with observable facts, excluding values, ideals, etc., is grounded on the *normative* claim that knowledge *ought to* conform to a particular ideal model—i.e., the model of what is taken for "scientific" observation. Thus a model of what knowledge *ought to be* is employed to establish what knowledge *is*. The paradox is intensified when it is argued, on this foundation, that knowledge cannot deal with *normative* questions but must confine itself to determining what *is* the case. An ideal model of knowledge is thus tacitly invoked to support the view that knowledge cannot determine the validity of ideal models.

PAGE 20 Some philosophers, like Gilbert Ryle, have claimed that the "stock use," or commonly accepted use, of words supplies a norm of correct use. The trouble is that accepted linguistic uses are often ambivalent and sometimes conflicting. Thus ordinary use allows us to talk about *mind* in various ways, either as an unobservable psychic entity or as a physiological process attendant upon observable behavior. In *The Concept of Mind*, Ryle argued that the former way of speaking is incorrect. While professing to be guided by ordinary language, what Ryle does is to invoke non-linguistic considerations to discredit one form of ordinary language in favor of another form.

PAGE 20 Austin, "A Plea for Excuses," in Chappell, *Ordinary Language*, p. 49.

PAGE 22 Whitehead, *Adventures of Ideas*, ch. XV, sec. 2.

PAGE 22 Aristotle, *Poetics*, XXII; 1459a.

PAGE 22 The metaphor of the mind as wax on which impressions are stamped goes back to Plato (*Theaetetus*, steph. 191-96). It is also used by Aristotle (*De Anima*, III, iv). In John Locke's *Essay Concerning Human Understanding* the metaphor is that of "white paper, void of all characters" (bk. 2, ch. I, sec. 2). The metaphor, in either form, stresses the *receptivity* of mind to impressions or imprintings.

PAGE 23 As to the *optical* or *visual* model of mind, see Jonas, *The Phenomenon of Life*, pp. 135-56. The optical model combines the idea of receptivity with the idea of detachment or distance. Marcel has characterized existentialism as a revolt against the "mode of thought which has become incarnate in optical metaphors" in *Man Against Mass Society*, p. 40. John Dewey also attacked the optical model because of its tendency to produce a "spectator theory of knowledge" in *The Quest for Certainty*, ch. I.

PAGE 23 White, *Medieval Technology and Social Change*, p. 125.

PAGE 23 Richards, *The Philosophy of Rhetoric*, p. 94.

PAGE 24 Imagination viewed as a form of pretending: see Ryle, *The Concept of Man*, ch. VIII.

PAGE 25 Richards, *The Philosophy of Rhetoric*, p. 92.

Chapter 3

General Note: Many writers are concerned today with the connection between the deterioration of language and the lowering of standards in politics, ethics, and the arts. There has been little attention paid, however, to the misuse of metaphors and models as a contributing factor. Several examples in this chapter involve confusions due to shifting models or to the use of unspecified or unrecognized models.

PAGE 27 Mumford, *Technics and Human Development*, p. 96. Although Mumford's earlier works, such as *Technics and Civilization*, are justly praised, some of his more recent works, notably *Technics and Human Development*, 1967, and *The Pentagon of Power*, 1970, reflect serious misapplications of a governing model, namely the model of the *machine*. Because modern society is wedded to machines and because some social institutions are *like* machines in their regularity and precision, Mumford tries to argue that modern technical society *is* a vast machine—in his words a "megamachine." But the analogy breaks down at a crucial point. A machine like a clock or an engine does not deform or distort its constituent parts; it depends rather upon the parts' functioning naturally according to their normal properties. To the extent that a human bureaucracy can enslave or deform the individuals who live under it, the bureaucracy is *unlike* a machine. Mumford tries, in effect, to *literalize* a metaphor, and thereby confuses the issues.

PAGE 28 Commentaries on McLuhan are noted in Coser, "The Intellectual as Celebrity," *Dissent*, Winter 1973.

PAGE 29 Marcuse, *Man Against Society*, p. 88.

PAGE 30 MacIntyre, *Herbert Marcuse: An Exposition and a Polemic*, p. 70.

PAGE 32 Quinton, in Morris, *Freedom and Responsibility*, p. 514.

PAGE 32 Hart, *Punishment and Responsibility*, pp. 5-6.

PAGE 32 Orwell, *A Collection of Essays*, pp. 163, 177.

PAGE 34 Frankel, *The Love of Anxiety and Other Essays*, Delta ed., pp. 129-30.

PAGE 35 Camus, *The Rebel*, pp. 283-84.

PAGE 36 Adams, *The Education of Henry Adams*, ch. IV; Dewey, *Democracy and Education*, ch. X, XIV.

PAGE 37 Schacht, *Alienation*, Anchor ed., pp. 245-46.

PAGE 38 Becker, *Beyond Alienation*, p. 88.

PAGE 38 Heinemann, *Existentialism and the Modern Predicament*, pp. 10-11.

PAGE 39 In the *Communist Manifesto* Marx satirized the use of the expression "alienation of humanity."

PAGE 39 For the development of different meanings of the word "revolution" see Arendt, *On Revolution*, ch. I. As to the wide variety of modern meanings, see Ellul, *Autopsy of Revolution*.

PAGE 40 Oglesby, *Containment and Change*, pp. 147-48. Emphasis in the original.

PAGE 41 Morgan, *The Human Predicament: Dissolution and Wholeness*, pp. 320-21, 325.

PAGE 42 Tocqueville, vol. 2, in the chapter on Language and Literature. Abridged version, (ed.) Commager, p. 289.

Chapter 4

General Note: Useful discussions of the classical Greek views of man and the world may be found in Finley, *Four Stages of Greek Thought*; Dodds, *The Greeks and the Irrational*; and Snell, *The Discovery of the Mind*. Jaeger's great three-volume work, *Paideia*, is comprehensive.

PAGE 45 It is a clear mistake to assume, as some writers do, that the religious doctrine of a special divine creation served to separate man from nature. The doctrine of special divine creation applied to the whole of nature, including man.

PAGE 46 Aristotle, *Politics*, bk. 1, ch. II.

PAGE 46 Whitehead, *Adventures of Ideas*, ch. IX, sec. 4.

PAGE 47 Jonas, *The Phenomenon of Life*, Delta ed., pp. 188-210.

PAGE 48 Whitehead, *Adventures of Ideas*, ch. XI, XIV, XV, holding that all perspective awareness is "clothed with emotion" and that "the notion of mere knowledge is a high abstraction." Whitehead emphasizes the fact that the great Greek philosophers never separated cognitive awareness from feeling and emotion.

PAGE 48 A representative and influential modern treatment was Ralph Barton Perry's *General Theory of Value*, 1926. Perry defined value as "any object of any interest," but he identified *interest* with attitudes of favor or disfavor, approval or disapproval. The result was to deny that cognitive concerns, such as curiosity or wonder, constitute *interests*. This special sense of the word *interest* is reflected and perpetuated in phrases like "disinterested curiosity" (often applied to scientists). The fact is that the impartial concern of the scientist is a sophisticated form of human *interest* with strong emotive overtones. See Polanyi, *Personal Knowledge* and *The Study of Man*.

PAGE 50 *Prometheus Bound*, lines 441-44. Edith Hamilton's translation is available in *Three Greek Plays*, W. W. Norton, 1937.

PAGE 51 I have chosen to render the Greek word as *hybris* rather than the more familiar *hubris*. For the Greek tragedians, *hybris* suggested aspiring to do or think things beyond the proper limits of what human beings should do or think. See Jones, *On Aristotle and Greek Tragedy*, pp. 86ff, 166ff. Its opposite was knowing and observing the limitations of the human condition.

PAGE 51 *Oedipus Rex*, lines 872-82. Cavander's translation is available in *Sophocles*, (ed.) Corrigan, Laurel edition, Dell Publishing Co., 1965.

PP. 52-53 Jonas, *The Phenomenon of Life*, pp. 175-82; also Harvanek, "The Community of Truth," *International Philosophical Quarterly*, March 1967, p. 70.

Chapter 5

PAGE 56 The most impressive modern spokesman for legal positivism and the so-called *command theory* of law is Hans Kelsen. Although Kelsen denies the objectivity of *ethical* norms, he insists that *legal* norms can be objectively established, that their existence can be empirically determined for any given society, and that the effect of a duly enacted law is not merely to *describe* conduct but to impose an obligation—i.e., to generate an *ought*. See Kelsen, *General Theory of Law and the State*. He also argues persuasively that the idea of descriptive causal laws (as generally employed in the sciences) is itself derived historically from the earlier idea of *responsibility* imposed by *prescriptive decrees*. See Kelsen, *What Is Justice?* pp. 303-49.

PAGE 56 Olafson's book, *Principles and Persons*, is valuable on many counts, including his attempt to "translate" some of the basic terminology of the best known existentialist philosophers into more familiar language, thereby making many issues more comprehensible.

PAGE 56 Rousseau, *First and Second Discourses*, p. 114, St. Martin's Press ed.

PAGE 57 Rousseau, *First and Second Discourses*, p. 25, St. Martin's Press ed. (quoted by the editor from another work of Rousseau).

PAGE 57 Quotations from *The Social Contract* are from bk. 2, ch. III, and bk. 1, ch. VI. As to the two aspects of Rousseau's position, see Cassirer, *The Question of Jean-Jacques Rousseau*.

PAGE 58 As to the ambiguities of the old distinction between *nature* and *convention*, see Dodds, *The Greeks and the Irrational*, p. 182ff.

PAGE 58 Becker, *Beyond Alienation*, p. 254.

PAGE 59 Murchland, *The Age of Alienation*, p. 130.

PAGE 59 Whitehead, *Adventures of Ideas*, ch. IV, sec. vii.

Chapter 6

General Note: Rieff has analyzed perceptively the *ethical* implications of the Freudian view of man. See especially Chapter IX of Rieff, *Freud: The Mind of the Moralist*. As to the *ethical* implications of Marx's historical determinism, see Selsam, "The Ethics of the Communist Manifesto," *Science and Society, A Centenary of Marxism*, Winter 1948 (for a Marxist view), and Camus, *The Rebel*, Part III, sec. 5 (for an anti-Marxist view). I have not found any discussion of the ethical implications of Skinner's views.

PP. 63-64 May, *Love and Will*, pp. 183 and 197.

PAGE 64 Rieff, *Freud: The Mind of the Moralist*, ch. X; Rieff, *The Triumph of the Therapeutic*, ch. V-VIII.

PAGE 64 Fromm, *Psychoanalysis and Religion*, pp. 73-98.

PAGE 64 On the theory that intellectual curiosity must be explained in terms of libido or aggression, see McClelland in *The Ecology of Human Intelligence*, pp. 309-41.

PAGE 65 "On 'Having' a Poem," *Saturday Review*, July 15, 1972.

PAGE 68 Chomsky, "A Review of B. F. Skinner's *Verbal Behavior*," *Language*, XXXXV, 1959.

PAGE 68 Skinner, "On 'Having' a Poem."

PAGE 68 Skinner, *Beyond Freedom and Dignity*, p. 204.

PAGE 69 Whitehead, *The Function of Reason*, ch. I.

PAGE 69 Epicurus, *Letters, Principal Doctrines and Vatican Sayings*, p. 68.

PAGE 69 Skinner, *Beyond Freedom and Dignity*, p. 213.

PP. 70-71 The distinction between giving an *explanation* of a belief and establishing its *validity* is readily illustrated: if a child believes in Santa Claus, his belief is explained causally by the fact that his parents told him of Santa Claus. But this circumstance does not show that his belief is true. A general *causal* theory of behavior, like Skinner's, serves to explain *all* types of belief, including Skinner's own. But since it explains all possible beliefs, valid and invalid alike, it can supply no basis for distinguishing between those that are warranted and those that are not. To distinguish between views which are sound and views which are unsound requires criteria of *evaluation*. If all evaluative judgments are excluded—as Skinner's view seems to contemplate—then we cannot evaluate Skinner's theories or those of his opponents. We cannot say that Skinner is right because, in his view, judgments of rightness and wrongness have no standing of their own. They are merely psychological *events* to be explained but not subject to critical evaluation.

PAGE 71 For a discussion of Sartre, see Olafson, *Principles and Persons*.

PAGE 71 Marx quotations are from *Capital and Other Writings*, ed. Eastman, Modern Library, 1932, pp. 1, 8.

PAGE 72 Drucker, *The End of Economic Man*, pp. 45-46.

PAGE 73 Potter, *People of Plenty*, ch. VIII.

PAGE 73 As to current versions of Marxism, with a critical analysis by a writer of radical sympathies, see Mills, *The Marxists*. For differing views concerning the "humanism" of Marx's early writings and their compatibility with existentialism, see Novack, *Existentialism vs. Marxism*.

Chapter 7

PP. 75-76 Peirce, *Essays in the Philosophy of Science*, pp. 196-97.

PAGE 76 The characterization of Dewey is by Smith, *The Spirit of American Philosophy*, p. 116.

PAGE 77 That linguistic descriptions presuppose norms for the activity of describing; Cavell, *Must We Mean What We Say?* p. 22.

PP. 77-78 Vickers, *Value Systems and Social Process*, ch. VIII, pp. 178-79, in Pelican ed. It should be noted that Vickers speaks here only about the act of judging that an *accepted norm* applies to a specific case. He does not discuss the kind of ethical judgment involved when an accepted norm is itself evaluated in the light of some *ideal norm*. I would note the importance of distinguishing the two situations, which are usually lumped together as if they were the same. When we evaluate an action by applying an accepted norm, the situation is essentially similar to that which arises when a general description of any kind is judged to apply to a particular case. When, however, we are evaluating our own accepted evaluations—i.e., when we are testing accepted norms against ideal norms—we run the risk of an infinite regress unless we can find an *ultimate norm* to which we can appeal. I suggest that the ultimate norm is supplied by an *ideal model of man.*

PAGE 78 Cassirer, *The Philosophy of Symbolic Forms,* vol. 2, p. 31.

PAGE 78 Boulding, *The Image,* pp. 25-26.

PAGE 79 Jonas, *The Phenomenon of Life,* p. 158.

PAGE 79 On teaching language to a chimpanzee, see Premack, "Teaching Language to an Ape," *Scientific American,* Oct. 1972. Note that the experiments described do not suggest that the ape could either *invent* a symbol or *invent* ways of teaching it to humans. By contrast, the inventiveness of the human experimenters in devising ways to teach some of their symbols to the ape was remarkable.

PP. 81-84 Whitehead, *Science and the Modern World,* ch. I, p. 22, Mentor ed.

PAGE 84 Hanson, *Observation and Explanation,* p. 5.

Chapter 8

PAGE 88 Whitehead, *Adventures of Ideas,* ch. XV, sec. iii.

PP. 88-99 Whitehead, *Adventures of Ideas,* ch. IX, sec. v.

PAGE 89 Allport, *Personality and Social Encounter,* ch. I.

PAGE 92 For a discussion of the textual problems in *Job,* see Pfeiffer, *Introduction to the Old Testament,* part 5, ch. III.

PAGE 92 Orwell, "Inside the Whale," *Collection of Essays,* pp. 241-42.

PAGE 92 Camus, *The Rebel,* Vintage ed., p. 101.

PAGE 93 Cf. Kuhn, *The Structure of Scientific Revolutions,* on changes of scientific "paradigms" and resistance thereto.

PAGE 94 Marcus Aurelius, *Meditations,* bk. 8, sec. 52, trans. Long.

PAGE 94 Erikson, *Identity, Youth, and Crisis,* pp. 31, 33.

PP. 94-95 Frankl: the first quotation is from Frankl, *The Will to Meaning,* p. 27. The second (longer) quotation is from Frankl, *From Death Camp to Existentialism,* p. 97.

PAGE 95 Lifton, *Boundaries,* p. 16. Cf. Lifton, *Death in Life: Survivors of Hiroshima.*

PAGE 95 Lifton, *Boundaries,* p. 54. Cf. Lifton, *Revolutionary Immortality.*

General Note: Although the word *meaning* is customarily applied to symbols such as words, its metaphorical extension to human existence is familiar. Witness the famous speech in *Macbeth,* Act V, Scene IV, which concludes with the assertion that life is "a tale told by an idiot, full of sound and fury, signifying nothing."

READER'S GUIDE

References to standard works, available in many editions, are omitted in the Reader's Guide (for example, works by Aristotle, Descartes, Rousseau, and Plato). The Notes provide sufficient information for finding these references.

Adams, Henry. *The Education of Henry Adams.* Boston: 1918. Riverside Press, Sentry ed., 1961.

Allport, Gordon W. *Personality and Social Encounter.* Boston: Beacon Press, 1964.

Arendt, Hannah. *The Human Condition.* Chicago: University of Chicago Press, 1958.

——. *On Revolution.* New York: Macmillan, 1963. Viking Compass ed., 1965.

Austin, J. L. "A Plea for Excuses," *Proceedings of the Aristotelian Society, 1956-57,* Vol. LVII: reprinted in Chappel, V. C. (ed.), *Ordinary Language.* Englewood Cliffs, New Jersey: Prentice-Hall, 1964.

—— *How to Do Things with Words.* Cambridge: Harvard University Press, 1962.

Becker, Ernest. *Beyond Alienation.* New York: George Braziller, 1967.

Black, Max. *Models and Metaphors.* Ithaca: Cornell University Press, 1962.

Boulding, Kenneth. *The Image.* Ann Arbor: University of Michigan Press, 1956.

Burckhardt, Jacob. *The Civilization of the Renaissance in Italy.* Published originally in German, 1860. (Various English editions are available.)

Camus, Albert. *The Rebel,* trans. Bower. New York: Knopf, 1956. Vintage ed., 1956.

Cassirer, Ernst. *An Essay on Man.* New Haven: Yale University Press, 1944.

——. *The Logic of the Humanities,* trans. Howe. New Haven: Yale University Press, 1961.

——. *The Philosophy of Symbolic Forms,* trans. Manheim. 3 vols. New Haven: Yale University Press, 1957.

——. *The Question of Jean-Jacques Rousseau,* trans. Gay. Bloomington: Indiana University Press, 1963.

Cavell, Stanley. *Must We Mean What We Say?* New York: Scribner's, 1969.

Chomsky, Noam. "Review of B. F. Skinner's *Verbal Behavior,*" *Language,* XXXXV, 1959, pp. 26-58. Reprinted in Fodor and Katz (eds.), *The Structure of Language.* Englewood Cliffs, New Jersey: Prentice-Hall, 1964.

Cohen, Yehudi A. *Man in Adaptation.* 3 vols. Chicago: Aldine, 1971.

Coser, Lewis. "The Intellectual as Celebrity," *Dissent,* Winter 1973.

Dewey, John. *The Quest for Certainty.* New York: Minton, Balch, 1929.

——. *Democracy and Education.* New York: Macmillan, 1916. Paper ed., 1961.

Dodds, E. R. *The Greeks and the Irrational.* Berkeley: University of California Press, 1951.

Drucker, Peter. *The End of Economic Man.* New York: John Day, 1939.

Eisenberg, Leon. "The *Human* Nature of Human Nature," *Science,* April 14, 1972.

Ellul, Jacques. *Autopsy of Revolution,* trans. P. Wolf. New York: Knopf, 1971.

Epicurus. *Letters, Principal Doctrines and Vatican Sayings.* New York: Bobbs-Merrill. Liberal Arts ed., 1964.

Erikson, Erik H. *Identity, Youth and Crisis.* New York: W. W. Norton, 1968.

Ferkiss, Victor C. *Technological Man: The Myth and the Reality.* New York: Braziller, 1969. Mentor ed., New American Library, 1970.

Finley, John H., Jr. *Four Stages of Greek Thought.* Stanford: Stanford University Press, 1966. (The Harry Camp Lectures for 1965.)

Frankel, Charles. "Four Illusions of Foreign Policy," *N.Y. Times Magazine,* reprinted in Frankel, *The Love of Anxiety and Other Essays,* New York: Dell, Delta, 1967.

Frankl, Viktor E. *From Death Camp to Existentialism.* Boston: Beacon Press, 1959. (Later reissued with some emendations of Part II under the title *Man's Search for Meaning,* Washington Square Press, 1963.)

————. *The Will to Meaning.* New York: New American Library, 1970.

Fromm, Erich. *Psychoanalysis and Religion.* New Haven: Yale University Press, 1950. Paper ed., 1959.

————, and Ramon Xirau (eds.). *The Nature of Man.* New York: Macmillan, 1968.

Fuller, Lon L. *The Morality of Law.* New Haven: Yale University Press, 1964.

Hanson, Norwood Russell. *Observation and Explanation.* New York: Harper & Row, 1971.

Harré, Rom. *The Principles of Scientific Thinking.* Chicago: University of Chicago Press, 1970.

Hart, H. L. A. *Punishment and Responsibility.* Oxford: Oxford University Press, 1968.

Hartnack, Justus. *Wittgenstein and Modern Philosophy,* trans. Cranston. New York: Doubleday, Anchor, 1965.

Heinemann, F. H. *Existentialism and the Modern Predicament.* London: Adam and Charles Black, 1953. American edition, revised, New York: Harper Torchbooks, 1958.

Heschel, Abraham J. *Who Is Man?* Stanford: Stanford University Press, 1965. (West Lectures for 1963.)

Jaspers, Karl. *Way to Wisdom: An Introduction to Philosophy,* trans. Manheim. New Haven: Yale University Press, 1960.

————. *The Future of Mankind,* trans. Ashton. Chicago: University of Chicago Press, 1961.

————. *Man in the Modern Age,* trans. Paul. London: Routledge & Kegan Paul, 1951. American ed., New York: Doubleday, Anchor, 1957.

Jonas, Hans. *The Phenomenon of Life.* New York: Harper & Row, 1966. Delta ed., 1968.

Jones, John. *On Aristotle and Greek Tragedy.* New York: Oxford University Press, 1962.

Kelsen, Hans. *General Theory of Law and the State,* trans. Wedberg. Cambridge: Harvard University Press, 1945. Republished, New York: Russell & Russell, 1961.

————. *What Is Justice?* Berkeley: University of California Press, 1960.

Kramer, Hilton. "The Age of the Avant-Garde," *Commentary,* Oct. 1972.

Krimerman, L. I., & L. Perry (eds.). *Patterns of Anarchy.* New York: Doubleday, Anchor, 1966.

Kuhn, Thomas S. *The Structure of Scientific Revolutions.* Chicago: University of Chicago Press, 1962. Second ed., enlarged, 1970.

Lifton, Robert Jay. *Boundaries.* New York: Random House, Vintage, 1970.

————. *Revolutionary Immortality.* New York: Random House, Vintage, 1968.

————. *Death in Life: Survivors of Hiroshima.* New York: Random House, 1967. Vintage ed., 1969.

Lipset, M. L., *Revolution and Counterrevolution.* New York: Basic Books, 1968. Revised ed., Doubleday, Anchor, 1970.

Lipset, M. L., & G. M. Schaflander. *Passion and Politics: Student Activism in America.* Boston: Little, Brown, 1971.

MacIntyre, Alasdair. *Herbert Marcuse: An Exposition and A Polemic*. New York: Viking, 1970.

McClelland, D. C. "On the Dynamics of Creative Physical Scientists," in *Contemporary Approaches to Creative Thinking*, (ed.) Gruber et al. Reprinted in *The Ecology of Human Intelligence*, (ed.) Hudson. Harmondsworth, Middlesex, England: Penguin, 1970, pp. 309-41.

Marcel, Gabriel. *Man Against Mass Society*, trans. Fraser. American ed., Chicago: Regnery, 1962.

———. *Problematic Man*, trans. Thompson. American ed., New York: Herder & Herder, 1967.

———. *Three Plays*, trans. Heywood and Gabain. New York: Hill & Wang, Dramabook, 1965.

Marcuse, Herbert. *One-Dimensional Man*. Boston: Beacon Press, 1964.

———. "Repressive Tolerance," in Wolfe, Moore & Marcuse, *A Critique of Pure Tolerance*. Boston: Beacon Press, 1965.

May, Rollo. *Love and Will*. New York: W. W. Norton, 1969.

Mills, C. Wright. *The Marxists*. New York: Dell, 1962.

Monod, Jacques. *Chance and Necessity*, trans. Wainhouse. New York: Knopf, 1971. Vintage ed., 1972.

Morgan, George W. *The Human Predicament: Dissolution and Wholeness*. Providence: Brown University Press, 1968. Delta ed., 1970.

Mumford, Lewis. *Technics and Civilization*. New York: Harcourt, Brace & World, 1934. Harbinger ed., 1963.

———. *Technics and Human Development*. New York: Harcourt, Brace, Jovanovich, 1967.

———. *The Pentagon of Power*. New York: Harcourt, Brace, Jovanovich, 1970.

Murchland, Bernard. *The Age of Alienation*. New York: Random House, 1971.

Novack, George. *Existentialism vs. Marxism*. New York: Dell, 1966.

Oglesby, Carl. "Vietnamese Crucible," in Oglesby & Shaull, *Containment and Change*. New York: Macmillan, 1967.

Olafson, Frederick A. *Principles and Persons*. Baltimore: Johns Hopkins University Press, 1967.

Orwell, George. *A Collection of Essays*, including "Politics and the English Language" (pp. 162-77) and "Inside the Whale" (pp. 215-56). New York: Doubleday, 1954.

Peirce, Charles S. *Essays in the Philosophy of Science*. (ed.) Tomas. New York: Bobbs-Merrill, 1957.

Pepper, Stephen C. *World Hypotheses*. Berkeley: University of California Press, 1942.

Pfeiffer, Robert H. *Introduction to the Old Testament*. New York: Harper & Brothers, 1941.

Platt, J. R., ed. *New Views of the Nature of Man*. Chicago: University of Chicago Press, 1965.

Polanyi, Michael. *Personal Knowledge*. Chicago: University of Chicago Press, 1958.

———. *The Study of Man*. Chicago: University of Chicago Press, 1963.

Potter, David. *People of Plenty*. Chicago: University of Chicago Press, 1954.

Premack, Ann and David. "Teaching Language to an Ape," *Scientific American*, October 1972.

Quinton, A. M. "On Punishment," Analysis XIV (1954), pp. 1933-42. Reprinted in Herbert Morris, *Freedom and Responsibility*, pp. 512-17. Stanford: Stanford University Press, 1961.

Reichenbach, Hans. *The Rise of Scientific Philosophy*. Berkeley: University of California Press, 1951.

Revel, Jean-François. *Without Marx or Jesus*, trans. Bernard. New York: Doubleday, 1971.

Richards, I. A. *The Philosophy of Rhetoric*. Oxford: Oxford University Press, 1936. Galaxy ed., 1965.

Ricoeur, Paul. *The Symbolism of Evil*, trans. Buchanan. New York: Harper & Row, 1967. Beacon Press ed., 1969.

Rieff, Philip. *Freud: The Mind of the Moralist*. New York: Viking Press, 1959, Anchor ed., 1961.

——. *The Triumph of the Therapeutic*. New York: Harper & Row, 1966. Harper Torchbook ed., 1968.

Ryle, Gilbert. *The Concept of Mind*. London: Hutchinson, 1949. American ed., New York: Barnes & Noble, 1949.

Schacht, Richard. *Alienation*. New York: Doubleday, 1970. Anchor ed., 1971. (Introductory Essay by Walter Kaufman.)

Selsam, Howard. "The Ethics of the Communist Manifesto," *Science & Society,* Winter 1948.

Simon. Yves R. *Philosophy of Democratic Government*. Chicago: University of Chicago Press, 1951. Phoenix Books ed., 1961.

Skinner, B. F. *The Behavior of Organisms*. New York: Appleton-Century, 1938.

——. *Walden Two*. New York: Macmillan, 1948; paper ed., 1962.

——. *Beyond Freedom and Dignity*. New York: Knopf, 1971.

——. "On 'Having' a Poem," *Saturday Review*, July 15, 1972.

Smith, John E. *The Spirit of American Philosophy*. Oxford: Oxford University Press, 1963.

Snell, Bruno. *The Discovery of the Mind*, trans. Rosenmeyer. Cambridge: Harvard University Press, 1953. Harper Torchbook ed., 1960.

Thucydides. *Peloponnesian War*. References are to Galaxy ed., Oxford Press, (ed.) Sir Richard Livingstone.

Tocqueville, Alexis de. *Democracy in America*. Abridged edition, (ed.) Commager. New York: Oxford University Press, 1947.

Urmson, J. O. *Philosophical Analysis*. Oxford: Oxford University Press, 1956.

Vickers, Geoffrey. *Value Systems and Social Process*. Hammondsworth, England: Penguin Books, 1970.

White, Lynn, Jr. *Medieval Technology and Social Change*. Oxford: Oxford University Press, 1962. Paper ed., 1964.

Whitehead, Alfred North. *Science and the Modern World*. New York: Macmillan, 1925. Many later editions.

——. *The Function of Reason*. Princeton: Princeton University Press, 1929. Beacon ed., 1958.

——. *Adventures of Ideas*. New York: Macmillan, 1933. Many later editions.

INDEX

ABOUT THE AUTHOR

A specialist not only in metaphysics, but also in the philosophy of law and in ethical and political theory, Professor Emeritus Philip H. Rhinelander became a philosophy professor by a circuitous route. He received his B.A. in classics and philosophy *summa cum laude* from Harvard University in 1929; he then received his L.L.B. from Harvard Law School in 1932 and practiced law in Boston for eight years. During World War II he served as a lieutenant commander in the United States Naval Reserve. Following the war, he returned to Harvard, where he completed his doctorate in philosophy (1949) and was appointed to the teaching staff in philosophy and general education.

Undergraduate education holds a particular interest for Professor Rhinelander. He served as Director of General Education at Harvard, and in 1956 he joined Stanford University as Dean of the School of Humanities and as a professor of both philosophy and the humanities. In 1961, he resigned his deanship to devote his full time to teaching. In 1963 Professor Rhinelander was the recipient of Stanford's highest honor for faculty, the Lloyd W. Dinkelspiel award for distinguished service to undergraduate education.